HARVARD STUDIES IN ENGLISH

VOLUME IX

THE SONGS OF THOMAS D'URFEY

BY

CYRUS LAWRENCE DAY

LONDON : HUMPHREY MILFORD

OXFORD UNIVERSITY PRESS

THOMAS D'URFEY

From the portrait by van der Gucht. Reproduced by permission of Baron Sackville

THE SONGS OF
THOMAS D'URFEY

SELECTED AND EDITED

BY

CYRUS LAWRENCE DAY

CAMBRIDGE · MASSACHUSETTS

HARVARD UNIVERSITY PRESS

1933

PRINTED AT THE HARVARD UNIVERSITY PRESS
CAMBRIDGE, MASS., U.S.A.

PREFACE

THOMAS D'URFEY was the most prolific dramatist and the most popular lyric poet of his age; and he was the friend and entertainer of no less than five English monarchs. To-day his reputation has suffered an eclipse, and "the famous comic poet" (for so the newspapers described him when he died in 1723) is known chiefly through the pages of Addison, Steele, and Pope, or perhaps as the editor of the collection entitled *Pills to Purge Melancholy*.

Most of D'Urfey's writings deserve the oblivion into which they have fallen. But not so his best songs and ballads. For in his day he achieved a kind of preëminence in the field of popular lyric poetry; and, moreover, many of his songs have definite value and interest on their own account.

This edition aims to provide accurate texts of the words and music of the most meritorious, the most popular, and the most typical of D'Urfey's once well-known songs. The facts of his life are summarized in the Introduction, while the Notes contain a bibliographical account of each of the twenty-six songs reprinted.

No study of D'Urfey could be brought to completion without access to the collections of the Harvard College Library, the Yale University Library, the Bodleian Library, and the British Museum. To the officers of these institutions I wish to express my gratitude for many courtesies extended to me.

My chief indebtedness is to Professor Hyder Edward Rollins, whose friendship has stimulated my interest in scholarship, and whose learned advice has been indispensable in my work on D'Urfey.

C. L. D.

NEWARK, DELAWARE
April 18, 1933

CONTENTS

LIST OF FACSIMILES

THE SONGS OF
THOMAS D'URFEY

INTRODUCTION

I. LIFE

THOMAS D'URFEY was born in Devonshire, perhaps at Exeter,[1] about 1653.[2] Little is known of his parentage except that he was of mixed French and English stock, and that he claimed kinship with the noble family of D'Urfé in France.[3]

His father, Severinus D'Urfey, was a grandnephew, according to Steele,[4] of Honoré d'Urfé, the celebrated author of *L'Astrée*. Disinherited for the "Extravagancy of his Youth," or for some other reason unknown to Steele, Severinus came to England, and proved himself "excellently well gifted in all Gentleman-like Qualities, tho' undoing all by his immoderate Vice of Gaming." I have been unable to find any reference to Severinus in the annals of the D'Urfé family, and it may be that his descent was illegitimate. Chetwood's assertion that D'Urfey's father was a Huguenot who fled from La Rochelle in 1628

1. Chetwood (*The British Theatre*, 1750, p. 101) is the first biographer to specify Exeter. In 1930 I searched the extant parish registers of Exeter, but failed to find D'Urfey's name, or any record of his family. The archives of the Devon and Cornwall Record Society, which Mr. H. Tapley Soper, librarian of the Exeter City Library, kindly permitted me to examine, yielded similar negative results.

2. An epitaph on D'Urfey, printed in *Miscellaneous Poems, by Several Hands*, 1726, p. 6, is the only early authority for this date. It gives his age when he died as three score years and ten, a figure that must be regarded as only approximately correct.

3. See the titles of his two translations from Honoré d'Urfé in *A New Collection of Songs and Poems*, 1683, pp. 61, 73.

4. *The Lover*, No. 40, May 27, 1715.

has been accepted by nearly all biographers, but is un-
supported by documentary evidence, and is very im-
probable. Several writers, including J. W. Ebsworth in
the *Dictionary of National Biography*, have tried to clear
away the chronological difficulties by assuming the refugee
to be D'Urfey's grandfather instead of his father. But
even when thus amended, Chetwood's account is far less
plausible than Steele's. For the D'Urfé's in France were
uniformly orthodox in religion, and, furthermore, Steele was
personally acquainted with D'Urfey, and wrote during his
lifetime. The suggestion of William Oldys[1] that D'Urfey
only pretended to be allied to the house of D'Urfé is worth
noting.

Steele informs us that D'Urfey's mother was a gentle-
woman of Huntingtonshire, of the family of the Marmi-
ons; but Ebsworth's inference that she was related to
Shackerley Marmion, the dramatist, is unfounded. In
September, 1698, D'Urfey wrote a hymn to his mother
"*at* Cullacombe," and printed it in *New Operas*, 1721,
pages 356–357. Since D'Urfey's Cullacombe promised
almost certainly to be identical with the farm Collacombe
Barton in the parish of Lamerton, Devon,[2] I visited that
parish in 1930. With the courteous aid of the Rev. G. L.
Edwards I had the good fortune to turn up the record of
the burial of "Mrs ffrances Durfey" in the parish register
of St. Peter's Church, Lamerton, under the date September 29, 1702. The family of Nicholas Rowe came from
Lamerton, while Collacombe Barton, an attractive Elizabethan manor house, was at that time owned by the locally

1. MS. notes to Langbaine (Addit. MS. 22593, fol. 35ᵛ).
2. See J. E. B. Gover, A. Mawer, and F. M. Stenton, *The Place-Names of Devon*, part I, p. 185 (English Place-Name Society, vol. VIII, Cambridge, 1931), for variant forms and spellings.

important Tremaine family, with whom Mrs. D'Urfey
appears to have been living in 1698.

Of D'Urfey's youth and education we know nothing except that he probably did not attend either of the universi-
ties. Langbaine[1] declares that he "was first bred to the
Law," but at least three contemporary documents[2] ac-
cuse him of having begun life in a much more humble
capacity — as a scrivener's apprentice. In this connection
it may be pertinent to note that a certain John Durfey
was "Stacioner at the Gate" for Lincoln's Inn in 1665,
with an allowance of four shillings a week,[3] and that this
is the only other occurrence of the name "Durfey" I
have found. Can this John have had any connection with
our Tom and his career as a scrivener? It is tempting to
believe so.

Not long after he reached his majority, D'Urfey quit
the law, or whatever profession he was then following,
and became "a Knight Errant in the Fairy Land of
Poetry";[4] but his first exploits were not especially successful. *The Siege of Memphis*, an insufferably bombastic
heroic play, was produced in September, 1676, several
years after *The Rehearsal* had made heroic plays ridiculous.
He then published a curious work called *Archerie Reviv'd;
Or, The Bow-Man's Excellence*, written in collaboration
with Robert Shatterel, or Shatteral, an elderly actor, and
dedicated to the king and queen. *Archerie Reviv'd* is
nothing more nor less than a versification of Ascham's

---

1. *An Account of the English Dramatick Poets*, 1691, p. 179.
2. *Wit for Money*, 1691, p. 5; *The Sessions of the Poets*, 1696, p. 12; and
Sloane MS. 1009, *ca.* 1683, fol. 154.
3. *The Records of the Honourable Society of Lincoln's Inn* (The Black Books),
1889, III, 47–48.
4. *Bussy D'Ambois*, 1691, dedication.

Toxophilus, with Ascham's learned references to Pliny, Herodotus, Xenophon, and other ancients impressively adorning the margins. The concluding regulations for holding archery contests, which were popular and numerous at this time, are filched verbatim from James Partridge's *Ayme for Finsburie Archers*, 1628.

On November 4, 1676, D'Urfey's first comedy, *Madam Fickle*, was produced at the Dorset Garden Theater, and was very much applauded by Charles II and the Duke of Ormonde, who attended the play together. Ormonde at once drew D'Urfey from his impecunious retirement and presented him to the king — and from that moment D'Urfey's career may be said to have commenced.

Neither his demeanor nor his aspect were calculated to ingratiate him with Charles. He stuttered excessively (except when singing or swearing), and he was so confused when in the presence of his monarch that he was unable to utter a single word, even his own name.[1] His appearance was as grotesque as his manner.[2] His ponderous, crag-like forehead towered above thick, arched eyebrows and cavernous brown eyes. His nose was enormous, colossal — sharp and hooked like the beak of some huge bird of prey — as monstrous a nose, assuredly, as ever Cyrano was cursed with. His lips were thin, and as he grew older, worldly sensual lines began to harden round them. Protruding lantern jaws supported the whole physiognomy and gave to their unfortunate owner a half-

---

1. Contemporary allusions to his stuttering are very numerous. As to his embarrassment in the presence of Charles II, see *Wit and Mirth: Or Pills to Purge Melancholy*, 1719, I, 338.

2. His portrait hangs at Knole, in Kent, and is reproduced with jocular comments in *Portraits of the British Poets*, 1824, II, No. 88, and also as the frontispiece for the present volume.

melancholy, half-ferocious aspect, ill-suited to his character as a humorist.

But he had other qualities which more than made up
for his external deficiencies. He had a resonant bass
voice, and an inimitable talent for composing and singing
witty songs of the kind Charles liked best to hear. Charles's
taste in music was notoriously shallow. He was a lover of
"slight songs," reports Roger North,[1] and was unable to
endure any music to which he could not beat time with
his foot. One of his mistresses, little Molly Davis, seems
first to have attracted him by her charming performance of "My lodging it is on the cold ground," which
"Rais'd her," says Downes,[2] "from her Bed on the Cold
Ground, to a Bed Royal." It was just this sort of ballad
that D'Urfey knew so well how to indite. He had, furthermore, a vulgar, impudent wit, and a good-natured willing-
ness to play the buffoon — to be the butt of a jest as well
as the author of one.

Accordingly, Charles was pleased to make the young
poet one of the privileged intimates of his lighter
moments. "I myself," says Addison,[3] "remember King
Charles the Second leaning on *Tom d'Urfey's* Shoulder
more than once, and humming over a Song with him."
Addison, to be sure, can hardly have been an eye-witness
to scenes of this sort, for he was only a boy when Charles
died, but the authenticity of his picture is confirmed by
the title of the song "Advice to the City," [4] which was
"*so remarkable*," D'Urfey boasts, "*that I had the Honour to
Sing it with King* Charles *at* Windsor; *He holding one part*

1. *The Musical Grammarian*, ed. Hilda Andrews, 1925, pp. 27-28.
2. *Roscius Anglicanus*, 1708, p. 24.
3. *The Guardian*, No. 67, May 28, 1713.
4. *Wit and Mirth: Or Pills to Purge Melancholy*, 1719, I, 246.

of the Paper with Me." The titles of many other songs in D'Urfey's early collections record the names of the places where he entertained the court, and it is clear that at Whitehall, Winchester, Newmarket, Windsor, and the houses of the nobility, — in fact, wherever the king went, whether on business or pleasure, — D'Urfey was generally one of his attendants.

Ormonde also continued to be kind to him, as we learn from several dedications and poems; and so did Christopher Monck, second Duke of Albemarle. Albemarle was a lavish host at New Hall, his seat in Essex, and often had D'Urfey there to entertain his guests. Among several allusions to his protection of D'Urfey may be cited the following passage from a contemporary *Satyr on the Poets*, 1680, contrasting the splendor of New Hall with the wretchedness of D'Urfey's apartments in London:

> D——*fy* that rhimes as Squirril jingle Bells,
> For sonnets fam'd as far as *Epsom* Wells;
> That prates and talks for Almonds like a Parret,
> Sings Roundelays and Stanza's in a Garret;
> If he does sometimes keep his Carnaval,
> To make their Graces merry at *New-hall*,
> All after that is Lent, and Penury:
> Even *Joseph Hindmarch* now has laid him by, }
> And vows he ne'er will trade in's poetry. }
> Thus hopeless Pence from Epick Bays to drain,
> *Jockey* and *Moggy* makes him eat again.[1]

---

1. I have not been able to find the source of these lines, but a leaf on which they are printed is prefixed to a copy of Winstanley's *Lives of the most Famous English Poets*, 1687, in the British Museum (shelf-mark C. 45. d. 13). They are clearly the original of the three-line jingle quoted by Whincop (*A Compleat List of all the English Dramatic Poets*, 1747, p. 225) and by subsequent biographers.

D'Urfey describes New Hall at some length in a panegyrical poem [1] which he wrote when Albemarle was appointed governor-general of Jamaica in 1687.

A Compleat Collection of Mr. D'Urfey's Songs and Odes, 1687, and *Bussy D'Ambois,* 1691, are dedicated to Edward Howard, Earl of Carlisle, in terms of some familiarity. This relationship survived the Revolution of 1688, and on March 28, 1690, D'Urfey's name appears as a servant of Carlisle's in a list of parliamentary protections entered in the office of the sheriff of Middlesex.[2] George, Earl of Berkeley, the Duchess of Grafton, and Charles, Lord Morpeth, also favored him. But he seems never to have insinuated himself very successfully into the good graces of James II, despite many valiant efforts to do so by means of songs, panegyrics, and dedications. James, indeed, was of a temper too saturnine for the frivolous pleasures that had diverted his more volatile brother.

While thus occupied as a sort of semi-official court jester and singer, D'Urfey did not cease writing for the stage. *A Fond Husband,* acted in May, 1677, was honored by the presence of Charles on three of the first five nights,[3] and was afterwards frequently revived until as late as 1740. *The Fool Turn'd Critick,* 1678 (perhaps acted as early as November, 1676), *Trick for Trick,* 1678 (a revision of Fletcher's *Monsieur Thomas*), *Squire Oldsapp,* 1679, *The Virtuous Wife,* 1680, *Sir Barnaby Whigg,* 1681, *The Royalist,* 1682, *The Injur'd Princess,* 1682 (a revision of *Cymbeline*), *A Common-Wealth of Women,* 1685 (from Fletcher's *The Sea Voyage*), *The Banditti,* 1685, and *A Fool's Prefer-*

---

1. *New Poems,* 1690, pp. 187–204.
2. *Historical Manuscripts Commission. Thirteenth Report, Appendix, Part V* (The Manuscripts of the House of Lords, 1690–1691), 1892, p. 12.
3. Addison, *The Guardian,* No. 82, June 15, 1713.

ment, 1688 (from Fletcher's *A Noble Gentleman*), complete
the list of his plays acted and published during the reigns
of Charles and James. Thirteen plays in as many years
is a remarkable record; and D'Urfey still had a long and
productive career ahead of him.

Between 1681 and 1683 D'Urfey entered the political
arena with four satires on Shaftesbury and the Whigs, who
were at that time seeking to exclude the Duke of York
from the succession to the throne. *The Progress of Honesty*, 1681, is an imitation of *The Poet's Complaint of his
Muse* (often attributed to Otway). It is written in the
irregular Pindaric stanzas popularized by Cowley and
usually restricted to eulogies and elegies, and it was regarded highly enough to be reissued in 1681 and also,
in somewhat revised form, in 1739. *Butler's Ghost: Or,
Hudibras the Fourth Part*, a surprisingly sympathetic continuation of Samuel Butler's famous burlesque, followed
in 1682. D'Urfey turns Hudibras into a Whig, and paints
scathing portraits of such notorious and notable figures
as Titus Oates ("Doctoro"), Slingsby Bethel ("Stalli-
ano"), Shaftesbury ("Pygmy"), and others. *Scandalum
Magnatum*, also written in 1682, owes its inspiration in
form and manner to *Absalom and Achitophel* and *The
Medal*, but it deals with a later phase of Shaftesbury's
trial than either of Dryden's satires. Shaftesbury appears
as Prince Potapski (from the tap, or drain, in his unhealed
wound), and the *mis-en-scène* is Poland (in imitation of
the biblical setting of *Absalom and Achitophel*). The action
hinges upon Shaftesbury's prosecution of Graham and
Craddock, both of whom had been witnesses against him
in the government's attempt to indict him for high treason
in 1681. D'Urfey's last satire during this period was *The

Malcontent, an ineffective continuation of *The Progress of Honesty.* Though dated 1684, the term catalogues show that it was published late in the preceding year.[1]

In 1688, a momentous year for D'Urfey, Ormonde and Albemarle died, and the Revolution ousted the political party upon which he had hitherto depended for his bread and butter. For a few months, consequently, his future was in doubt, and he had to turn his hand to anything that would bring in money. He spent the summer of 1689 as a singing teacher at Josias Priest's boarding-school for girls in Chelsea, a position for which he must have been morally very unfit. While there he wrote an epilogue [2] for *Dido and Aeneas,* an opera by Tate and Purcell, which the young ladies of the school presented. How long he remained in this delightful lotus-land it is impossible to say, but long enough to collect the material for *Love for Money: Or, The Boarding School,* 1691, a comedy which anticipates the sentimentality of Cibber and Steele. The shameless satire of Priest and his school in this comedy gave much offense. Some of the characters were evidently drawn from life, and even the painted scene represented Chelsea, though D'Urfey maintained in his preface that it might just as well have been York. *Wit for Money: Or, Poet Stutter,* 1691, a clever attack on *Love for Money,* voices the opinion of D'Urfey's "hissing Antagonists," and may be from the pen of no less a pamphleteer than Tom Brown. It contains a deal of information about D'Urfey, most of it nowhere else available.

Another money-making project was a newspaper called *Momus Ridens: Or, Comical Remarks on the Publick Re-*

1. *The Term Catalogues,* ed. Edward Arber, 1905, II, 47.
2. *New Poems,* 1690, pp. 82–83.

ports, published every Wednesday, and consisting of facetious comments in verse upon the latest news, national
and international. It probably began on October 29, 1690,
and continued for twenty weeks until March 11, 1691.
Only five numbers of the paper seem to be extant: Nos.
3, 12, 16, 17, and 18, for November 12, 1690, and January
14, February 11, 18, and 25, 1691. Two lines of No. 20
are quoted in *Wit for Money* (page 4), which says that
D'Urfey abandoned the undertaking after receiving his
profits from the third night of *Love for Money*. As a
forerunner of the efforts of Addison and Steele to pur-
vey entertainment rather than news in periodical form,
Momus Ridens has a certain importance in the history of
journalism.

About this time, D'Urfey again turned to satire and
wrote a series of political poems, all but one of which he
published anonymously. *Collin's Walk through London
and Westminster*, the earliest of these, is dated 1690. Like
Butler's Ghost, it is a successful imitation of *Hudibras*, but
the objects of his ridicule are now a burly Jacobite major
of the Catholic faith, and a bumpkin named Collin, who
is a Presbyterian. The ill-assorted pair journey to London from the country and pass from one amusing situation
to another, with appropriate comments on the follies of
the age.

In 1691 D'Urfey attacked Dr. William Sherlock in three
pamphlets entitled *The Weesils*, *The Weesil Trap'd*, and
The Moralist. Sherlock, perhaps the most eminent non-
juror, took the oaths of allegiance to William and Mary
in 1691, and was at once appointed dean of St. Paul's.
Charges of inconsistency and avarice were hurled at him
in a hundred squibs and pasquinades, among which

D'Urfey's three poems are not the least effective. Although anonymous, and often thought to be by Tom Brown, all three are attributed to D'Urfey in *Wit for Money* (pages 3–7), and the first two are attributed to him also in the diary of Abraham de la Pryme under the date October 17, 1697:

I was this day with a bookseller at Brigg, who was apprentice to one who printed that scurrilous pamplet against Sherlock intitled the "Weesils," (the author of which was Durfee). He says that [he] is certain that his master got about 800 *l* by it. He says that Durfee was forced to write an answer to it which he entitled the "Weesel Trapped." [1]

Further evidence is supplied by *The Sessions of the Poets*, 1696 (page 11), which asserts that D'Urfey "never wrote a good Poem in his Life, except a scurrilous one against a Reverend Doctor of the Church." The reference can hardly be to anything but *The Weesils*. Finally, D'Urfey quotes eleven lines from *The Weesils* in the preface to his play *The Campaigners*, 1698.

The two weasel pamphlets go back to Aesop's fables and Reynard the Fox for their satirical inspiration. Sherlock is called Weesilion, and the blame for his sudden change of front is given to his ambitious wife, who brings pressure to bear upon him for worldly reasons. Between the two weasel poems came *The Anti-Weesils*, possibly by Brown, attacking the point of view of *The Weesils*.

His fourth satire in 1691 is *The Triennial Mayor*, in which Sir Thomas Pilkington, formerly satirized as Piltonski in *Scandalum Magnatum*, is now highly lauded. This satire is also anonymous, but it is ascribed to D'Urfey

1. *The Diary of Abraham de la Pryme*, ed. C. Jackson, 1870, p. 159.

by the author of *Wit for Money* (page 4), and by John
Dunton, who gives the impression that he suggested the
subject of the piece. "There is stuttering D'Urfey," he
complains,[1] "will scarce own who bid him write 'The
Triennial Mayor.'"

The Canonical States-man's Grand Argument Discuss'd,
1693, may also be D'Urfey's. It is directed against the
pamphleteering divine, Samuel Johnson, and in both form
and manner is a close imitation of *The Weesils*. Johnson
and his wife (called Goosilion and Goosiliana) argue much
as do Weesilion and his wife in *The Weesils*. D'Urfey's
last satire, *The Dog and the Otter: A Fable*, — an attack
upon Jeremy Collier, — is printed with *The Campaigners*,
1698. Later satires which have sometimes been ascribed
to D'Urfey are probably in all cases spurious.

D'Urfey's songs, like his satires, show that he transferred
his political allegiance to the Whigs as soon as the success
of William's *coup d'état* was assured. Already in June,
1689, we find him entertaining Queen Mary at Kensington
with a song entitled "The Scotch Virago," [2] a semi-political
trifle on General Hugh Mackay's expedition into the
Highlands against the Scottish Jacobites. His efforts to
sing himself into the favor of the new monarchs, indeed,
were numerous. On November 4, 1689, just twelve months
after the landing at Torbay, he addressed an ambitious
birthday ode [3] to William; but he never sang serious
pieces of this kind himself, and probably was not as yet

---

1. *The Life and Errors of John Dunton*, 1818, I, 86.
2. *New Poems*, 1690, pp. 183–185.
3. *Ibid.*, pp. 180–183. *The London Gazette*, No. 2503, November 7, 1689,
notes that the king's birthday "was celebrated at Court, with an Excellent
Consort of Music, Vocal and Instrumental; and a Ball at night, where the
Nobility and gentry appeared in extraordinary Splendor."

personally known to the king. For the queen's birthday
on April 30, 1690, he wrote an ode ¹ which was set to music
by Henry Purcell, and sung by Boucher, Roberts, Turner,
and Damascene,² all well-known singers of the day. Several other songs and odes for William and Mary are included in *Wit and Mirth: Or Pills to Purge Melancholy.*

Whincop ³ reports that King William had Tom sing to
him one night, "and a Gentleman, who was commanded to
accompany his Voice with his Instrument, told me very
lately, that the King laughed very heartily, and ordered
him a Present." No better proof of D'Urfey's skill as
an entertainer could be found; for William was not usually appreciative of foolery like D'Urfey's, nor did he
have leisure for recreation of any kind during his trou-
bled reign.

The poet himself imagined that he was solidly estab-
lished in the favor of the new monarchs and their court.
It seems hardly credible, but he actually considered himself entitled to the laureateship, which had just been
awarded to his rival Shadwell. In his *Poem Panegyrical*
on Albemarle, he attacks Shadwell as Og, the name formerly given to him by Dryden, and reveals his disappoint-
ment in the following lines:

> Forgive me Sir, that I these Truths relate,
> And believe Flattery is a thing I hate;
> The Courtier's Gloss to varnish his dull Speech,
> Could I have flatter'd well I had been Rich:
> A well form'd Parasite's an Art so dear,
> I might have got three hundred Pound a year.⁴

---

1. *Wit and Mirth: Or Pills to Purge Melancholy*, 1719, I, 62–64.
2. MS. Mus. c. 26, fols. 70–94ᵛ (Bodleian).
3. *A Compleat List of all the English Dramatic Poets*, 1747, p. 225.
4. *New Poems*, 1690, p. 203.

In *Mr. Haines's Second Recantation* he expresses his jealousy again. The words are put into the mouth of Haines, but it is D'Urfey who is speaking:

> Wits there are too, but Poet there's but one,
> A huge unweildy jarring Lute and Tunn,
> That spite of all my Parts the Laurel won.[1]

The earlier stages of D'Urfey's quarrel with Shadwell, a quarrel which began in 1681 with *The Progress of Honesty* and *Sir Barnaby Whigg*, have been ably set forth by Professor A. S. Borgman,[2] and need not be rehearsed in their entirety here. It may be well to repeat, however, that Sir Barnaby is a caricature of Shadwell and not of Shaftesbury, as has been rather absurdly suggested. One other matter should also be mentioned. The allusions in the prologue to Shadwell's *Bury Fair*, 1689, to the "*wretched* Poetitos, *who got praise For writing most* confounded Loyal Plays," and to the "*silly* Grubstreet *Songs worse than* Tom Farthing," were taken by D'Urfey to have been aimed at him, and he tried with ill-concealed irritation to defend himself in the preface to his *New Poems*, 1690. The desultory quarrel between the two poets ended with Shadwell's death in 1692. Since "none but Devils damn [from] beyond the grave," D'Urfey forgave his opponent, and wrote a prologue for Shadwell's posthumous play, *The Volunteers*, 1693.

The vanity that nourished D'Urfey's aspirations to the laureateship was one of his most amusing failings. Like Dryden he thought it essential to his dignity as a poet and a gentleman to appear in public attended by a page, whose livery, if we may trust the author of *The Sessions*

1. *Ibid.*, p. 206.
2. *Thomas Shadwell: His Life and Comedies*, 1928, pp. 62–64.

of the Poets, 1696 (page 14), he was unable to pay for. An imaginary dialogue between Tom D'Urfey and the ghost of Tom Heywood, sometimes ascribed to Daniel Defoe,[1] makes fun of him for keeping a foot-boy, but he defends his practise by citing the example of Jonson and Richard Brome.

After 1683 he affected an apostrophe in his name in order to advertise his aristocratic French origin. Properly speaking, the spelling should be "Durfey," the form in which it appears on the title-pages of his early works, in the record of his burial, on the stone slab that marks his grave, in the record of his mother's burial, and in the letters of administration of his estate. Some doggerel verses "*occasioned by Mr.* Durfy's *adding an &c. at the End of his Name*" ring the changes on all the possible spellings:[2]

> *Jove* call'd before him, t'other Day,
> The Vowels, *U, O, I, E, A;*
> And discontented Consonants,
> Either of *England*, or of *France*,
> That seem'd to fill the Name unworthy
> Of fam'd *Tom Durfy*, or *De-Urfe*.
>
> Fierce in the Cause, the Letters spoke all,
> *Liquids* grew rough, and *Mutes* turn'd vocal;
> Those four proud Syllables alone
> Were silent, which kind Fate thought worthy
> To run so smoothly, one by one,
> In the great Name of *Thomas Durfy*.
>
> *N*, by whom Names subsist, declar'd
> To have no Place in this, was hard;
> And *Q* maintain'd 'twas but his Due
> Still to keep Company with *U*;
> So hop'd to stand, as well as he,
> In the great Name of *Tom. Durfy*.

1. *Visits from the Shades*, 1704–1705, II, 73–82.
2. Printed in *Miscellanea*, 1727, I, 73–77, and ascribed to Alexander Pope.

E show'd, a Comma ne'er cou'd claim
A Place in any *British* Name;
Yet making here a perfect Botch,
Thrusts your poor Vowel from his Notch:
Hiatus mihi valdè deflendus!
From which good Jupiter defend us;
Who'd sooner quit our Part in thee,
Than be no Part of *Tom Durfy.*

B, and *L*, swore Bl—d, and W—nds:
X, and *Z*, cry'd P—x, and Z—nds.
G swore by G—d, it shou'd not be,
And *W* wou'dn't lose, not he,
An *English* Letter's Property
In the great Name of *Tom. Durfy.*

P protested, puff'd, and swore,
He'd ne'er be serv'd so like a Beast,
He was a Piece of Emperor,
And made up half a Pope at least.
C vow'd, he'd frankly have releas'd
His double Share in *Cæsar Caius*,
For only one in *Tom Durfeius.*

I Consonant and Vowel too,
To *Jupiter* did humbly sue,
That of his Grace he'd make a Patent,
To turn the Name into good *Latin*:
For tho' without them ('twas most clear)
Himself cou'd ne'er be *Jupiter*,
Yet they'd resign that Post so high,
To be the Gen'tive of *Durfei.*

In short, the rest were all in Fray,
From *Chris-Cross*, to *Et Cætera:*
Ev'n they (meer Standers by) too mutter'd,
Dipthongs and Tripthongs swore and stutter'd
That none had so much Right to be
Part of the Name of stutt'ring *T——*
T—Tom—a—Ass D—Dur—f—fy.

Then *Jove* spake thus with Care and Pain
We form'd this Name renown'd in Rhyme,

Not thine immortal *Neuf-Germain*,
Cost studious Providence more Time,
Yet now, as then, You all declare,
From hence to *Ægypt* you'll repair,
And turn strange *Hieroglyphicks* there,
Rather than Letters longer be,
Unless i' th' Name of *Tom Durfy*.

Were you all pleas'd, yet what I pray
To other Letters cou'd I say?
What if the *Hebrew* next shou'd claim
To turn quite backwards *Durfy*'s Name?
Shou'd the *Greek* quarrel too, by *Styx*, I
Cou'd ne'er bring in Ψ, and Ξ:
Omicron and *Omega* from us
Wou'd each hope to be *O* in *Thomas?*
And all th' ambitious Vowels vie, ⎫
No less than *Pythagorick* Υ, ⎬
To have a Place in *Tom Durfy?* ⎭

Then well belov'd, and trusty Letters,
Cons'nants, and Vowels too, their Betters!
We, willing to repair this Breach,
And (all that in us lies) please each,
Et Cætera to our Aid will call;
Et Cætera represents you all:
Et Cætera therefore we decree, ⎫
For ever henceforth join'd shall be ⎬
To the great Name of *Tom Durfy*. ⎭

It was his desire to comport himself like a man of
fashion, I suppose, that led him to fight a duel with a
musician named Bell, presumably no very dangerous opponent. Tom Brown's verses are unfortunately our only
source of information concerning the episode:

The Epsom *Duel*, 1689.

I Sing of a Duel in *Epsom* befel,
'Twixt fa-so-la *Durfey*, and so-la-mi *Bell*:
But why do I mention the scribbling Brother?
For naming the one, you may guess at the other.

Betwixt them there happen'd a horrible Clutter,
Bell set up the loud Pipes, and *Durfey* did splutter.
Draw, *Bell*, wer't thou Dragon, I'll spoil thy soft Note,
Thy squeaking, said t'other, for I'll cut thy Throat.
With a Scratch on the Finger the Duel's dispatch'd,
Thy *Clineas* (Oh *Sidney!*) was never so match'd.[1]

Epsom and Tunbridge Wells were two resorts which he often visited and wrote about.

D'Urfey's pretensions seemed like the crassest sort of impudence to his Grub-Street rivals, but probably only amused his indulgent patrons. These were now as exclusively Whigs as they had formerly been Tories. Charles Montague, the munificent patron of Addison, Congreve, and Prior, was one. It was he who introduced D'Urfey to Queen Mary,[2] and it was at Montague House in 1696 or 1697, just before the Peace of Ryswick, that the song beginning "Loyal English boys"[3] was sung before King William, probably by D'Urfey himself. Philip Sidney, third Earl of Leicester, was another generous Maecenas to the poets of this age. D'Urfey was presented to him by Sir Charles Sedley, and thereafter became one of the fortunate wits who gathered every Saturday night at Leicester's board to dine, and drink, and entertain their host. He was also a frequent visitor at Penshurst, Leicester's historic country estate.

It was in the reign of William and Mary that he won his most conspicuous triumphs in the drama. In 1691 he brought out his sentimental comedy *Love for Money* and his revision of Chapman's *Bussy D'Ambois*. In 1692 came *The Marriage-Hater Match'd*, which was "plaid six

---

1. *The Remains of Mr. Tho. Brown*, 1720, p. 65.
2. *The Comical History of Don Quixote*, part III, 1696, dedication.
3. *Wit and Mirth: Or Pills to Purge Melancholy*, 1719, II, 92-95.

days together," and "met with very good success." [1] The actor Dogget is said to have performed the part of Solon in this play with inimitable skill. *The Richmond Heiress* was a comparative failure when acted early in 1693, but later in the year it was revived, and "Acted several times, with Alterations and Amendments." [2]

The first two parts of *The Comical History of Don Quixote* were acted in May and June, 1694, with immense success.[3] The dowager Duchess of Ormonde saw the first part in rehearsal, and "when the ladies came to my Third Day," boasts D'Urfey in his dedication, "there never was at this time o' th' year, in the Hemisphere of the Playhouse, so dazzling and numerous a Constellation seen before." The second part was even more enthusiastically acclaimed than the first. Queen Mary herself attended the play and was highly diverted by the comical dialogue in the fourth act. Doubtless much of the success was due to Purcell's music, and to the admirable cast — to say nothing of the help given by Cervantes. The third part of the *Don Quixote* trilogy was a failure when it was produced in November, 1695.[4]

Seven plays, none of them markedly successful, followed in rapid succession. *A Wife for any Man*, with incidental music by Jeremiah Clarke, was acted in 1696 or 1697, but never printed. *Cinthia and Endimion*, an opera, was performed April 5, 1697,[5] but it had been written some years

1. *The Gentleman's Journal*, February, 1692, p. 26.
2. *Ibid.*, April, 1693, p. 130, and November, 1693, p. 374.
3. *Ibid.*, May, 1694, p. 134, and June, 1694, p. 170. See also *The London Gazette*, No. 2989, July 5, 1694, for an advertisement of the publication of the first part and the songs for the second part.
4. W. Barclay Squire, "Purcell's Dramatic Music," *Sammelbände der Internationalen Musikgesellschaft*, 1904, V, 518.
5. Leslie Hotson, *The Commonwealth and Restoration Stage*, 1928, p. 377.

earlier, perhaps in 1685.[1] *The Intrigues at Versailles*, also acted in 1697, was a failure, though D'Urfey declares that it was read and approved by Betterton and Congreve. *The Campaigners*, 1698, was published with an angry preface in reply to Jeremy Collier, who had attacked the *Don Quixote* plays in his *Short View of the Immorality and Profaneness of the English Stage*. Collier's diatribe had at least one concrete result as far as D'Urfey was concerned, for the justices of Middlesex brought an indictment against him on May 12, 1698, for having written *Don Quixote*.[2] Congreve and the publishers Tonson and Briscoe were indicted at the same time, but the case does not seem to have been tried. The two parts of *The Famous History of the Rise and Fall of Massaniello*, acted in the spring of 1699, and *The Bath*, acted May 31 and June 9, 1701,[3] bring the total of D'Urfey's plays prior to the accession of Anne up to twenty-seven. Three only, of his remaining six plays, were put upon the boards.

The date of Queen Anne's accession marks the beginning of a rapid decline in D'Urfey's literary powers. He was in his fiftieth year in 1702, and his creative force was largely spent. He continued to pour forth a flood of loyal songs and odes, but his songs on Marlborough have little of his old spontaneity. In the drama, too, he had had his say,

1. Two songs from the play were printed in *The Theater of Music*, 1685, II, 9, 44, and D'Urfey himself declares in his dedication that it was written for an earlier occasion.

2. Narcissus Luttrell, *A Brief Historical Relation of State Affairs*, 1857, IV, 379. *Dawks's News-Letter*, No. 297, May 12, 1698, reports that on the last day of the sessions at the Old Bailey, "the Grand Jury of London delivered a Presentment against all Stage-Plays and Lotteries, (which tend so much to the corruption and Debauchery of Youth) and the Bench were pleased to say they would take the same into consideration."

3. Hotson, *The Commonwealth and Restoration Stage*, 1928, p. 379.

and he wrote only three plays during the reign of Anne: *The Old Mode & the New*, 1703, *Wonders in the Sun*, 1706, and *The Modern Prophets*, 1709. Farquhar's *The Recruiting Officer* was first acted on the third night of *Wonders in the Sun*, much to D'Urfey's financial inconvenience. *The Modern Prophets* is a satire on a group of religious enthusiasts known as the Camisard prophets. The death of the prince consort interfered with its being produced on the stage in 1708, and when it finally was acted on May 3, 1709, the Camisards had already been dispersed. For this reason it was a failure. It was the occasion, however, of some very witty essays by Steele in *The Tatler*.[1] Thomas Baker also took several flings at it, notably in the prologue to Mrs. Centlivre's *The Busy Body* and in *The Female Tatler*.[2]

D'Urfey enjoyed, after the turn of the century, several benefit performances of his early plays. Steele and Addison sponsored some of these,[3] and even Pope wrote a prologue "Designed for Mr. D'Urfey's Last Play." Pope's witty barbs can hardly have been much comfort to the unfortunate poet for whom the prologue was written:

> Grown old in Rhyme, 't were barbarous to discard
> Your persevering, unexhausted Bard:
> Damnation follows Death in other men;
> But your damn'd Poet lives, and writes again.
> Th' adventurous Lover is successful still,
> Who strives to please the Fair *against* her *Will:*
> Be kind, and make him in his Wishes easy,
> Who in your own *Despite* has strove to please ye.
> He scorn'd to borrow from the Wits of yore;
> But ever writ, as none e'er writ before.

---

1. Nos. 1, 4, 11, 43, April 12, 19, May 5, July 19, 1709.
2. Nos. 4, 8, 26, July 15, 25, September 5, 1709.
3. See, for example, *The Guardian*, Nos. 67 and 82, May 28 and June 15, 1713, and *The Lover*, No. 40, May 27, 1712.

You Modern Wits, should each man bring his Claim,
Have desperate Debentures on your Fame;
And little would be left you, I'm afraid,
If all your Debts to *Greece* and *Rome* were paid.
From his deep Fund our Author largely draws;
Nor sinks his Credit lower than it was.
Though Plays for Honour in old time he made,
'Tis now for better Reasons — to be paid.
Believe him, he has known the World too long,
And seen the Death of much immortal Song.
He says, poor Poets lost, while Players won,
And Pimps grow rich, while Gallants are undone.
Though *Tom* the Poet writ with ease and pleasure,
The Comic *Tom* abounds in other treasure.
Fame is at best an unperforming Cheat;
But 'tis substantial Happiness, *to eat.*
Let Ease, his last Request, be of your giving,
Not force him to be damn'd to get his Living.[1]

It was during the early part of Anne's reign that D'Urfey
wrote the thirteen narrative tales in prose and verse which
appear in *Tales Tragical and Comical*, 1704, *Stories Moral
and Comical*, 1706 (reissued 1707), and *New Operas*, 1721.
The variety of D'Urfey's tales is extraordinary, both with
respect to the meters in which they are written, and the
sources (French, English, Italian, and Greek) from which
they are derived. But their merit is exceedingly small.
Dryden's *Fables Ancient and Modern*, 1700, was the im-
mediate stimulus prompting their composition, as we learn
from the preface to *Tales Tragical and Comical*. D'Urfey
was always conscious of the genius of Dryden towering
above him, but he nowhere fell so far below his master as
in his tales. Despite their lack of merit, however, they had
a certain vogue among readers of light literature. Addi-

---

1. *The Poetical Works of Alexander Pope*, ed. A. W. Ward, 1924, pp.
469-470.

son [1] found a copy of one of the collections "Bound in Red Leather, gilt on the Back, and doubled down in several places" (the most indelicate passages, presumably), in the library of a fashionable lady who collected books only when she had heard them praised, or because she had seen the authors of them. Part of her library consisted of dummies of "All the Classick Authors in Wood."

Like her predecessors, Anne was appreciative of D'Urfey's histrionic and lyrical skill, and she frequently had him sing to her. Once she gave him fifty guineas, so it is said, for his lines ridiculing her rival, the aged Electress Sophia:

> The crown's far too weighty
> For shoulders of eighty;
> She could not sustain such a trophy;
> Her hand, too, already
> Has grown so unsteady
> She can't hold a scepter;
> So Providence kept her
> Away. — Poor old Dowager Sophy. [2]

Needless to say, the song was suppressed when Sophia's son, George I, came to the throne.

For some reason George was deaf to D'Urfey's lyrical blandishments. The elderly poet wrote many flattering odes to him, one of which, "Ocean's Glory," [3] was set by the renowned Dr. Pepusch, and designed for the coronation banquet. But the lord chamberlain prevented its performance — a high-handed procedure that provoked D'Urfey to write a stinging ditty upon him as Lord Scrape:

1. *The Spectator*, No. 37, April 12, 1711.
2. William Hone, *The Table Book*, 1828, II, 650.
3. *Wit and Mirth: Or Pills to Purge Melancholy*, 1719, I, 17–18.

> But great Lord Scrape *was a Winner*,
> *Some threescore Pounds, or more,*
> *For the King had no Musick at Dinner,*
> *The like never known before.*[1]

The kindness of the Prince and Princess of Wales made up for the neglect of the king. Chetwood [2] tells how "The late Secretary *Craggs*, by command of Queen *Caroline* when she was Princess, introduced *Tom* to her Highness then at *Richmond*, who was extremely pleased with his facetious Account of the former Reigns." Caroline, who had a mind of her own, possessed copies of the first two volumes of D'Urfey's *Songs Compleat, Pleasant and Divertive*, and a set of *Pills to Purge Melancholy*.[3] In 1714, 1715, 1716, and 1717, she attended the public theater with the prince, her husband, in order to hear D'Urfey deliver his annual orations on the times.[4] These always came about the first week in June, when the Jacobites, celebrating the anniversary of the restoration of Charles II on May 29, were likely to be most factious. As the birthday of George I fell on May 28, flattery of the new dynasty could be conveniently combined with an effort to allay the discontent of the supporters of the old.

Other patrons of his later years were William Bromley, Speaker of the House of Commons; Lionel Cranfield Sackville, seventh Earl and first Duke of Dorset, and Philip, Duke of Wharton. Bromley employed him as a singing-master for his daughter, and gave him the use of

---

1. *Ibid.*, II, 90.
2. *The British Theatre*, 1750, p. 101.
3. Now in the British Museum.
4. See *The Daily Courant*, Nos. 3937, 4246, 4557, and 4867, for June 7, 1714, June 3, 1715, May 29, 1716, and May 27, 1717: also *Wit and Mirth: Or Pills to Purge Melancholy*, 1719, I, 337 and 339; II, 313 and 317.

a lodge on his estate near where the "famous Bagington Castle" once stood. Dorset, a dissipated young man of low tastes, often entertained D'Urfey at Knole, his magnificent estate in Kent. He had the generous habit of putting new-minted guineas under the plates of his literary guests — a habit pleasing enough to D'Urfey, we may be sure. A portrait of D'Urfey, painted when he was advanced in years, still hangs at Knole, and shows him reading from a sheet of music, with some song-books under his arm. Wharton, who, like Dorset, was something of a libertine, inherited a fortune and in 1718 retired to his estate at Winchendon. Here he built a banqueting-house, Brimmer Hall, which is celebrated by D'Urfey in "A Health to his Grace the Duke of Wharton," [1] and in the dedication to Wharton of *New Operas*, 1721.

His closing years were marked by only a small number of new works. In 1719 he gathered together his remaining lyrics in the first two volumes of *Songs Compleat, Pleasant and Divertive* (reissued in the same year as *Wit and Mirth: Or Pills to Purge Melancholy*), and in 1721 he first published several longer pieces, including three unacted plays, in a volume called *New Operas*. According to Chetwood,[2] his final undertaking was a translation of *L'Astrée*, his illustrious kinsman's famous romance. I have not been able to verify Chetwood's assertion that proposals were printed for the publishing of this translation, although I have searched the newspapers of the period. Just prior to his death he may have lived in lodgings at Windsor.[3]

1. *New Operas*, 1721, p. 369.
2. *The British Theatre*, 1750, p. 101.
3. See *The Humourist*, 1725, II, 31, and the mock-affidavit appended to *The English Stage Italianiz'd*, 1727, a work which purports to be by D'Urfey but which is really spurious.

D'Urfey died in 1723, and was buried at the Duke of Dorset's expense on Tuesday, February 26, in St. James's Church, Piccadilly, at that time the most fashionable church in London. Above his grave is a stone in the south wall of the church with the simple inscription:

TOM DURFEY
Dyed Feb! y.ᵉ 26.ᵗ 1723

His burial was reported in all the newspapers of the day. Oldys, in his annotated copy of Langbaine,[1] says he left Steele his gold watch and diamond ring, but his assertion is probably based on an apocryphal legend of late date. Letters of administration of his estate were taken out on March 15 (Court of the Archdeacon of Middlesex). He was described as late of St. Martin's in the Fields in the county of Middlesex, bachelor,[2] and John Bates was his chief creditor. The following epitaph was printed in 1726:

> Here lyes the *Lyrick*, who with Tale and Song,
> Did Life to threescore Years and ten prolong:
> His Tale was pleasant, and his Song was sweet;
> His Heart was chearful — but his Thirst was great.
> Grieve, Reader, grieve, that he, too soon grown old,
> His Song has ended, and his Tale has told.[3]

II. Songs

The extraordinary popularity of D'Urfey's songs is a phenomenon that must be reckoned with in any comprehensive estimate of late seventeenth and early eighteenth-

1. British Museum: C. 28. g. 1.
2. Aitken (*The Life of Richard Steele*, 1889, II, 290) says that "James Lucas, Christ Church, London" was the surety; but the Principal Registry of the Probate, Divorce, and Admiralty Division of the High Court of Justice does not confirm his statement.
3. *Miscellaneous Poems, by Several Hands*, 1726, p. 6.

century literature. Better than any of his contemporaries, D'Urfey knew how to appeal to the taste of the average Englishman of his day. Nearly everybody was familiar with his ditties, and sang them with gusto upon appropriate occasions. Nearly everybody was familiar with the figure of the poet himself, either in the cities of London and Westminster, followed by his liveried servant,[1] or at the theater talking impudent nonsense with my lord,[2] or at Will's Coffee-House jesting and punning with the wits.[3] "Many an honest Gentleman has got a Reputation in his own Country, by pretending to have been in Company with *Tom. d'Urfey*," remarks Addison,[4] with benevolent irony; "he has been the Delight of the most Polite Companies and Conversations from the beginning of King *Charles* the Second's Reign to our present Times."

The learned world, to be sure, did not share the enthusiasm for D'Urfey's songs that was evinced by the nobility and gentry on the one hand, and the *mobile vulgus* on the other. Virtually every reference to him that I have encountered in the writings of his contemporaries is scornful. But this should not blind us to his importance as a lyric poet; for his popularity was, to the fastidious wits of his age, an unpardonable sin in itself. He was looked upon as a mere ballad-monger, as the successor of Thomas Deloney, William Elderton, and Martin Parker; and he was, therefore, beyond the pale of literary respectability. And yet the very critics who condemned his ballads most vociferously were not always on that account immune to

1. Steele, *The Lover*, No. 40, May 27, 1715.
2. Brown, *Amusements Serious and Comical*, 2d ed., 1702, p. 50.
3. *Oxford and Cambridge Miscellany Poems, ca.* 1704, p. 313.
4. *The Guardian*, No. 67, May 28, 1713.

their peculiar fascination. "The Town may da–da–damn me for a Poet," D'Urfey himself is said to have stuttered, "but they si–si–sing my Songs for all that." [1]

Pope's condescension is typical. D'Urfey's songs, he affirms in a letter written to Henry Cromwell in 1710, are all the rage among the half-illiterate justices of the peace and toping squires of the country:

> I have not quoted one *Latin* Author since I came down, but have learn'd without Book a Song of Mr. *Thomas Durfey*'s, who is your only Poet of tolerable Reputation in this Country. He makes all the Merriment in our Entertainments, and but for him, there wou'd be so miserable a Dearth of Catches, that I fear they wou'd (*sans ceremonie*) put either the Parson or me upon making some for 'em. Any Man, of any Quality, is heartily welcome to the best Toping-Table of our Gentry, who can roundly hum out some Fragments or Rhapsodies of his Works: So that in the same Manner as it was said of *Homer*, to his Detractors; What? Dares any Man speak against him who has given so many Men to eat? (meaning the Rhapsodists who liv'd by repeating his Verses) So may it be said of Mr. *Durfey*, to his Detractors; Dares any one despise him, who has made so many Men drink? Alas, Sir! This is a Glory which neither you nor I must ever pretend to. Neither you, with your *Ovid*, nor I with my *Statius*, can amuse a whole Board of Justices and extraordinary 'Squires, or gain one Hum of Approbation, or Laugh of Admiration! These Things (they wou'd say) are too studious, they may do well enough with such as love Reading, but give us your antient Poet Mr. *Durfey*! [2]

Even more illuminating proof of his vogue with the masses is found in the anonymous *Wit for Money*, 1691 (pages 11–12):

1. *The Fourth and Last Volume of the Works of Mr. Thomas Brown*, 1715, p. 117.
2. *Miscellanea*, 1727, I, 29–30.

What Song, What Lampoon, What Satyr, Or what Play, in short, can please the Town, but what is Coyn'd in your Mint? I can go no where, but like Air, you are still to be found. From *Wapping* to *Tuttlefields*, from *Southwark* to *Shoreditch*, you fill the Nations mouth. The trudging Carman whistles your harmonious Poetry to his Horse, the Glass Coach Beau whispers them to his senceless Nymph, the Grumbling *Jacobite* mutters them in Corners to his Abdicated Brethren, the Coffee-house Bard, his Nose Sadled with Spectacles, pores over your *Comical Remarks*, as much as on the no less divertive *Observator*. Your Ballads, when half asleep, from the Street, in a high Base and a low Treble, wish me a good rest when I can catch it. The Cookmaid and Scullion listen to them, and the very Coachman ingratiates himself to the antiquated Chamber-maid with them. They will not escape the quiet Nursery, for there they Rock *Baby* asleep. In *Guild-Hall*, some of the *Anti-New Raparees* exalt them up to the very Hustins, and from the Philistine *Goliah*, now make you their third *Giant*. I see them on every Post, and shoals of them at every Booksellers, and must for a while have abdicated the Playhouse, had I not as much Complaisance for them as I have had for some of the foregoing Comical Entertainments.

A glance at almost any of the song-books of the period will confirm the testimony of Pope and the author of *Wit for Money*. Thus the elaborate collections published toward the end of the century by Henry Playford and his competitors, as well as the various volumes of "mug-songs" dating from about 1715, contain an astonishingly large proportion of his compositions. Many of his favorite songs continued to be reprinted again and again, until near the end of the eighteenth century, in popular anthologies like *The Choice*, 1733, *The Hive*, 1726-1732, and *The Aviary*, ca. 1750. A few of the best-known — "Cold and raw," "From rosy bowers," "At Winchester was a wedding," and others — appear to have had a sort of con-

tinuous sub-literary currency right up to the time when
they were rediscovered by antiquarians like Percy and
Ritson. About 1700 or a little earlier, single songs, printed
from copper plates engraved by Thomas Cross and other
engravers, began to drive out the more pretentious song-
books, which had hitherto been financially profitable. A
great many single songs are preserved in the British
Museum, and among them D'Urfey's outnumber those of
any other author. And finally the ballad operas of the
second quarter of the century corroborate the rest of the
evidence. Of the sixty-eight airs in *The Beggar's Opera*,
for example, ten are named after D'Urfey's songs (airs
II, III, V, XIX, XXI, XXIX, XXXI, XXXXIII, LXIII,
and LXVI). Other ballad operas show a like proportion.

In the Notes to the present edition I have given some
indication of the triumphant careers of several of the songs
which I have reprinted. Among others that were popular
may be mentioned "When Harold was invaded" (which
was familiar in Kent until well into the nineteenth century),[1] "In January last on Munnonday at morn" (long
a favorite in Scotland), "Genius of England" (often sung
at concerts in the eighteenth century), "Blow, Boreas,
blow," "As soon as the chaos was turned into form,"
"Blowzabella, my bouncing doxie," "Jolly Roger Twangdillo," "Maiden fresh as a rose," "Of all the simple things
we do," "Since now the world's turned upside down,"
"Since times are so bad," "Would ye have a young virgin
of fifteen years," and "Ye nymphs and sylvan gods."
All these songs, and several others, have interesting his-
tories, and considerations of economy alone have prevented
me from reprinting them.

1. See *Notes and Queries*, 1st series, 1850, I, 247, 339.

D'Urfey's success, it must be admitted, was due in no small measure to the composers who set his songs to music. Foremost among them, of course, was Henry Purcell, who supplied part or all of the incidental music for eight of his plays: *The Virtuous Wife*, *Sir Barnaby Whigg*, *A Fool's Preferment*, *The Marriage-Hater Match'd*, *The Richmond Heiress*, and the three parts of *The Comical History of Don Quixote*. Purcell's accompaniments for some of D'Urfey's occasional songs, such as "The Yorkshire Feast Song" and the 1691 birthday ode to Queen Mary ("Arise, my Muse, and to thy tuneful lyre"), are among his most effective compositions. "The Yorkshire Feast Song" has been especially admired for its simplicity and homebred strength, and was the first piece to be published by the Purcell Society when that organization began its ambitious edition of *The Works of Henry Purcell* in 1878. It was originally sung on May 27, 1690, at a great banquet for the nobility and gentry of York at Merchant-Taylors Hall, and cost the amazing sum of £100 to perform.

"From rosy bowers where sleeps the god of love," a celebrated "mad song" from the third part of *Don Quixote*, was the last song Purcell set to music before he died. It was a favorite throughout the eighteenth century, and is heard occasionally to-day. On May 25 and June 29, 1704,[1] Leveridge sang it between the acts at revivals of *The Constant Couple* and *The Fatal Marriage*. It was printed, also, in a great many song-books and miscellanies.

1. See advertisements on these dates in *The Daily Courant*, Nos. 656 and 688. D'Urfey's songs were often used for the purposes of *entre-acte* entertainment at this time.

The names of nearly forty composers appear in the several collections of D'Urfey's songs. After Purcell, the most important are Dr. John Blow, John Eccles, Thomas Farmer, Jeremiah Clarke, Samuel Akeroyde, and Daniel Purcell. Moreover, D'Urfey often made use of old airs like *Green sleeves, Cavalilly man, Old Sir Simon the king, O London is a fine town,* and many others. He also wrote airs of his own, but of these I have been able to recover with certainty only two, the air for "How vile are the sordid intrigues of the town" (pp. 98–99), and the air for "The valiant Eugene," [1] which I have not reprinted. "Steer, steer the yacht" [2] he described as "Set to a Tune of my own," but the music has not survived. There is no authority for the attribution of any other extant tunes to D'Urfey; though it must be admitted that the titles of two or three of his pieces leave some doubt whether he composed both the words and music or the words only.

The variety of his songs is more remarkable, I think, than their number. It is true that he wrote nearly five hundred from first to last, but as his productive career lasted some forty or forty-five years, his annual output amounted to less than a dozen. On the other hand, he essayed every type of lyric known at the time, and even originated several of his own. Roughly his work can be divided into three main groups: political songs, court songs, and country songs. But the distinction is not always very rigid, and some of his best pieces are impossible to classify under any definite heading.

D'Urfey's political and satirical songs, represented in this edition by "Joy to great Caesar," "Let Oliver now

---

1. *Wit and Mirth: Or Pills to Purge Melancholy,* 1719, I, 205–207.
2. *Ibid.,* II, 139.

be forgotten," and "Farewell, my loved science, my former delight," belong to an old and popular form of literary expression. The earliest political ballad in the English language, a piece of work stylistically like many of D'Urfey's, dates from 1264, shortly after the battle of Lewes; but similar vernacular compositions were doubtless common at a much earlier date, perhaps before the Norman Conquest. After the invention of printing, and particularly in the seventeenth century, songs and ballads acquired unprecedented importance for political and satirical purposes. The influence of typical ballads like Martin Parker's "When the King Enjoys His Own Again," or Wharton's "Lilliburlero," can hardly be overestimated. When printed on a broadside and offered for sale in the streets, the political ballad performed the two major functions of the modern newspaper: it supplied both news and the interpretation of news — both the reporter's narrative and the editor's comment. The authors of street-ballads were usually obscure hacks; but many sophisticated writers, like Marvell and Denham, experimented with the form for purposes of satire and invective. There were none, however, who could rival loyal Tom D'Urfey in popularity, or who could so successfully interpret the temper of the age.

His chief forerunner as a writer of political songs was Alexander Brome, who died in 1666. Brome was the leading composer of Cavalier lyrics just prior to the Restoration, and possibly he edited two important anthologies of anti-Roundhead, or Rump, songs in 1660 and 1662. Both Brome's songs and the anonymous Rump songs exerted a powerful influence on D'Urfey's lyrical style, as D'Urfey himself was aware. There are complimentary

allusions to Brome in *A Fond Husband* (I. i, III. i),
Sir Barnaby Whigg (I. i), and the song of "The Church
Jockey." [1] In *The Royalist* one of the characters sings two
lines of a ballad by Brome ("'Tis not the silver nor gold
for itself"), and then Brome himself, impersonated by the
actor Bowman, is brought upon the stage to sing D'Urfey's
loyal songs, "The great Augustus like the glorious sun"
and "Now, now the Tories all must droop." Most of the
latter is borrowed from Francis Quarles.

One important difference between D'Urfey and Brome
should be noted. D'Urfey never had the courage to sup-
port the underdog, and transferred his allegiance successively from the Stuarts to William and Mary, and Anne,
and George. His later political songs, however, have little
of his characteristic force and vitality. After 1700 he
wrote health after health to Marlborough and invective
after invective against Louis XIV and the French. But
of these only one can be said to have merit, that beginning
"Fill every glass and recommend 'em," itself the basis
of Gay's "Fill every glass for wine inspires us" in *The
Beggar's Opera*. For the most part, the interest of his
later political songs has died with the occasions which
inspired them.

His country songs — a second distinct lyrical group —
have their roots even more firmly fixed in English soil.
Crude but lively, coarse but robust, these popular and
characteristic ballads are in the main current of native
lyrical tradition. Typically they deal with the wooings
and weddings of dairymaids and bumpkins, and the em-
phasis is often placed with disconcerting frankness upon
the details of sex relationship. There is nothing at all in

1. *Wit and Mirth: Or Pills to Purge Melancholy*, 1719, II, 66–67.

the way of a romantic return to nature in these pieces, but rather a more or less illusory attempt at realism. As a matter of fact, however, the lusty folk whose amours are portrayed — the Toms and Dicks and Dollies — are just as conventional as the Strephons and Chloes of the classical tradition, and, it may be added, just as free from moral restraint. "The Winchester Wedding," which will be found on page 112, is a fair enough specimen of the songs in this group.

Closely allied to his country songs are his dialect songs — Scotch, Welsh, and Irish — and his sport songs on fishing, hunting, and horse-racing. Some of the best are written in the pseudo-Scotch dialect popular at the time. "The night her blackest sables wore," for instance, is permeated with a genuine passion that one can hardly praise too highly. Its only fault is syntactical irregularity, which, however, is scarcely noticed when the song is sung to Thomas Farmer's melody. "Cold and raw" is another Scotch song which well deserves its immense and long-lasting popularity.

The group I have labeled court songs comprises D'Urfey's most conventional work. Here he was emulating the artificial style of Rochester, Sedley, and the other fashionable wits whose gay, dissolute verses determined the lyrical tone of the nation — or at least of the court — during the reign of Charles II and afterwards. Love, of course, is his usual topic, though his best piece in this kind is perhaps his "Dirge on Chrysostom" (page 69), an exquisite little song which was justly admired by Charles Lamb. His least happy efforts are also the most formal and pretentious — his two odes in honor of St. Cecilia's Day, for example, and his birthday odes for Queen Mary. Tom

Brown, his arch-rival, had these in mind when he penned
the following witty but brutal verses:

> *To Mr.* D'Urfey, *upon his incomparable Ballads,*
> *call'd by him Lyrick Odes.*
>
> I
>
> Thou Cur, half *French*, half *English* Breed,
>   Thou Mungrel of *Parnassus*,
> To think tall Lines, run up to Seed,
>   Should ever tamely pass us.
>
> II
>
> Thou write *Pindaricks*, and be damn'd!
>   Write Epigrams for Cutlers;
> None with thy Lyricks can be shamm'd
>   But Chamber-Maids and Butlers.
>
> III
>
> In t'other World expect dry Blows;
>   No Tears can wash thy Stains out;
> *Horace* will pluck thee by the Nose
>   And *Pindar* beat thy Brains out.[1]

Not all D'Urfey's songs deserve such severity, as any
one who takes the pains to read the specimens I have reprinted will, I think, agree. Hostile critics of his work
declare that it bears the trail of the serpent. But such
criticism is hardly just. Vulgar and frank no doubt he
often was, as in his very popular song called "The Fart;
Famous for its Satyrical Humour in the Reign of Queen
Anne." [2] But vulgarity and frankness should be dis-
tinguished from indecency and obscenity, in which he
offended no more and no less than his contemporaries.

1. *The Fourth and Last Volume of the Works of Mr. Thomas Brown*, 1715,
p. 110.
2. *Wit and Mirth: Or Pills to Purge Melancholy*, 1719, I, 28-32.

His outstanding fault is carelessness and slovenliness in matter of detail, not indecency, and not lack of lyrical feeling. His neo-classical contemporaries, of course, were much more concerned with polish and form than they were with depth of feeling. By way of excuse for his slipshod rhymes and meters, D'Urfey pleads that the irregularities disappear when his songs are sung.[1] His excuse has a good deal of validity, and one cannot too strongly assert that it is impossible to appreciate the flavor of a Restoration song unless the words and the music are studied together.

Consider, for example, the melancholy little tune of "Cold and raw." When we hear it we are carried back as if by magic to the England of a former age. Or consider the exuberant strains of Farinelli's ground. It is really surprising how this apparently commonplace sequence of notes enables us to recapture the feeling of excitement that must have prevailed when the loyal boys roared out "Joy to great Caesar" during the last days of the Stuart dynasty.

No very great skill in music is needed in order to be able to pick the melodies out on a piano. The bass parts, usually intended for the theorbo, bass-viol, or lyra-viol, may be disregarded; for the accompaniment is a matter of small consequence in a Restoration song. A word of caution, however, is necessary, in the case of two or three of the facsimiles. The chorus of "All you that either hear or read" is said to come first; but that statement is incorrect. Furthermore the last seven notes (two bars) of the chorus should be slurred for the word "sing." "Let Oliver now be forgotten" also offers one or two difficulties. The

---

1. *A Compleat Collection of Mr. D'Urfey's Songs and Odes*, 1687, dedication.

first six bars are repeated, the third and fourth lines being sung to the same notes as the first and second. In the seventh bar the first two notes (D and F), and in the tenth bar both notes (G and A), should be slurred, because lines five and six each lack a syllable.

"Sleep, sleep poor youth" is the only song that is at all fully scored. It is arranged as a duet between a shepherd and a shepherdess, with a symphony of flutes and a bass for a stringed instrument. The composer has made an effort to express the sense of the words in the music, and the result is pleasing. There is an interesting change from triple to quadruple time in the chorus.

It will be observed that the facsimiles of the music are usually reduced in size, and that they represent three different methods of printing the notes, corresponding to changes in the printing and publishing business that took place at the end of the seventeenth century. The earliest style has lozenge-shaped notes of the kind used in all the music books published by the house of Playford between 1650 and 1685. "Joy to great Caesar" (page 48) is printed in this way, as well as several other early songs. In 1687 an improvement called the "new tied note" was introduced by Moore, Clark, and Heptinstall in the first volume of *Vinculum Societatis*, licensed on June 8 of that year. Round notes were now for the first time used, as in modern music, and the crooks of quavers and semiquavers were for the first time joined. "Cold and raw" (page 105), from the second volume of *Comes Amoris*, 1688, is a page from one of the earliest music books ever printed with the "new tied note." [1]

1. Grove's *Dictionary of Music and Musicians*, 1928, IV, 255, says that it is the earliest.

About 1700 the use of movable type was largely abandoned, — in popular music, at any rate, — probably because of its cost. In its place the printing of music from engraved copper or pewter plates became very widespread, Walsh and Hare being the leading publishers of this kind of work. As engraved songs were seldom dated, it is generally impossible to tell even approximately when they were published. The three engraved single songs reproduced in this edition (pages 65, 91, and 97) probably date from after 1725, and I have preferred such comparatively late texts only because of the difficulty of interpreting the musical notes in *Wit and Mirth: Or Pills to Purge Melancholy*.

D'Urfey's songs are found in his plays and in the successive collections which he published from time to time between 1683 and 1721. A chronological list, with a few brief remarks, is herewith appended.

1. *A New Collection of Songs and Poems*, 1683. 8°. Fifty-four songs, occasionally with music, and a poem in heroic couplets.
2. *Choice New Songs*, 1684. Folio. Twelve songs with music.
3. *Several New Songs*, 1684. Folio. Eight songs with music.
4. *A Third Collection of New Songs*, 1685. Folio. Twelve songs with music.
5. *A Compleat Collection of Mr. D'Urfey's Songs and Odes*, 1687. 8°. Seventeen songs without music. Bound with No. 6.
6. *A New Collection of Songs and Poems*, 1687. 8°. Seventy-five songs without music. Bound with No. 5.
7. *New Songs Sung in The Fool's Preferment*, 1688. 4°. Appended to the play, with music by Henry Purcell.
8. *New Poems, Consisting of Satyrs, Elegies, and Odes*, 1690. 8°. Fifty-nine poems and songs without music.

9. *The Songs to the New Play of Don Quixote. Part the First*, 1694. Two editions were published, a quarto and a folio. Seven songs with music.

10. *The Songs to the New Play of Don Quixote . . . Part the Second*, 1694. Folio. Eight songs with music.

11. *New Songs in the Third Part of the Comical History of Don Quixote*, 1696. Folio. Nine songs with music.

12. *A Choice Collection of New Songs and Ballads*, 1699. Folio. Seven songs with music.

13. "The Songs in the 1st and 2nd Part of, *Massianello* of *Naples*." Entered in the term catalogues [1] for Easter, 1699, and advertised in *The Post Boy*, No. 658, June 27, 1699.

14. "The Second collection of new Songs and Ballads." Entered in the term catalogues [2] for Trinity, 1699, and advertised in *The Post Boy*, No. 658, June 27, 1699, where it is said to include "Jolly Roger Twangdillo" and "Come all, great, small, short, tall, away to stool ball." Two leaves of this collection are probably preserved in a miscellaneous book of music in the Harvard College Library (Mus. 512.23F*, fols. 607, 610). They contain "Celimene, pray tell me" and "Loyal English boys, sing and drink with pleasure."

15. "The Songs and Dialogues [in the play called] Wonders in the Sun, or the Kingdom of the Birds." Advertised as "this Day publish'd" in *The Daily Courant*, No. 1346, August 7, 1706.

16. *Musa et Musica*, 1710. A collection of eight engraved songs.

17. *Songs Compleat, Pleasant and Divertive*, 1719. Originally consisted of five octavo volumes edited by D'Urfey, his own songs being assembled in volumes I and II. The collection was reissued in the same year under the more familiar title *Wit and Mirth: Or Pills to Purge Melancholy*. A sixth volume was added in 1720.[3]

1. *The Term Catalogues*, ed. Arber, 1906, III, 124, 129.
2. *Ibid.*, III, 140.
3. See C. L. Day, "*Pills to Purge Melancholy*," *The Review of English Studies*, 1932, VIII, 177–184.

18. *New Opera's, with Comical Stories, and Poems, on Several Occasions, Never before Printed*, 1721. 8°. A collection of poems and plays, with a few songs.

The following songs, arranged alphabetically, are printed neither in his plays nor in his several collections.

1. "Cease, foolish mortals, to pursue vain joys." — Peter Motteux's *The Gentleman's Journal*, March, 1692, p. 9.
2. "Go vind the vicar of Taunton Dean." — *The Monthly Mask of Vocal Music*, December, 1710.
3. "In seventeen hundred and three told twice over." — *The Monthly Mask of Vocal Music*, August, 1706.
4. "Jemmy, known the chief of aw the northern breed." — A single-sheet edition in the British Museum (G. 309 [63]).
5. "Let sorrow find those that never could love." — *The Last and Best Edition of New Songs*, 1677, sig. B1ᵛ (said to be from *Madam Fickle*, and therefore perhaps D'Urfey's).
6. "More gay our splendid court of Hymen shone." — Motteux's *The Gentleman's Journal*, May, 1694, p. 134.
7. "No more, no more his brains possess." — Preserved with music by D. Purcell in the Harvard College Library (Mus. 512.23F*, fol. 294), and said to be from the first part of *Massaniello*.
8. "Obscure and clowdy did the day appear." — An elegy on Oldham in *The Works of John Oldham*, 1722, II, 201.
9. "Once more the great general home returns." — *A Pill to purge State-Melancholy*, 1715, p. 15.
10. "Phillis has such charming graces." — A single sheet edition in the British Museum (G. 303[3]). It is said to be from *The Campaigners* and therefore may be D'Urfey's.
11. "Sabina to her daughter dear." — *The Monthly Mask of Vocal Music*, July, 1704.
12. "She tells me with claret she cannot agree." — A single sheet edition in the Harvard College Library (25242.13*, fol. 100).

13. "Thus of old great Hannibal returned." — *The Monthly Mask of Vocal Music*, November, 1710.
14. "When Rome was in her glorious state." — An ode on Dr. Blow in *Amphion Anglicus*, 1700, pp. i–ii.
15. "Ye circum and uncircumcised." — A single sheet edition in the British Museum (G. 305[357]).
16. "Ye sons of th' earth, in vain you get." — From D'Urfey's *Stories Moral and Comical*, 1706, p. 69.

How many of D'Urfey's songs were circulated anonymously it is impossible to say. Doubtless a few are scattered through the song-books and miscellanies of the period. But D'Urfey was not the sort of person to relish anonymity, and it is therefore unlikely that much of his work was published without his name. The foregoing lists are, I believe, reasonably complete.

D'URFEY'S SONGS

I

The KING's Health: Set to Farinel's
Ground. In Six Parts.

The First Strain.

Joy to Great *Cæsar*,
   Long Life, Love and Pleasure;
'Tis a Health that Divine is,
Fill the Bowl high as mine is:
   Let none fear a Feaver,   5
But take it off thus Boys;
   Let the King Live for ever,
'Tis no matter for us Boys.

The Second Strain.

   Try all the Loyal,
   Defy all,   10
   Give denyall;
Sure none thinks his Glass too big here,
   Nor any *Prig* here,
   Or Sneaking *Whig* here,
   Of Cripple *Tony*'s Crew,   15
   That now looks blue,
   His Heart akes too,
   The *Tap* won't do,
   His Zeal so true,
   And Projects new,   20
   Ill Fate does now pursue.

First Strain.

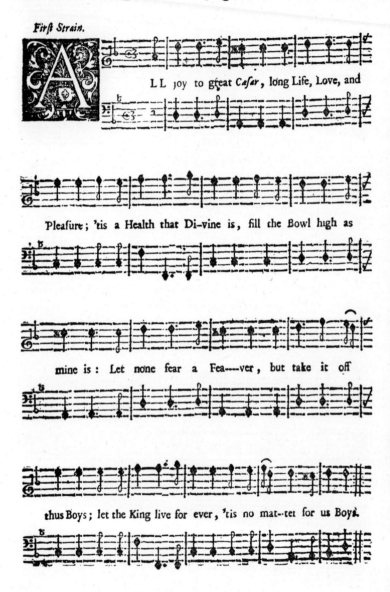

A LL joy to great *Cæsar*, long Life, Love, and

Pleasure; 'tis a Health that Di-vine is, fill the Bowl high as

mine is: Let none fear a Fea----ver, but take it off

thus Boys; let the King live for ever, 'tis no mat-ter for us Boys.

TRY all the Loy—al, de——fy all, give de—ni—al; sure

none thinks the Glass too big here, nor a——ny *Prig* here, or sneaking

Whig here, of Crip-ple *To-ry's* Crue, that now looks blue, his

Heart akes too, the Tap won't do, his Zeal so true, and

Projects new, ill Fate does now pursue.

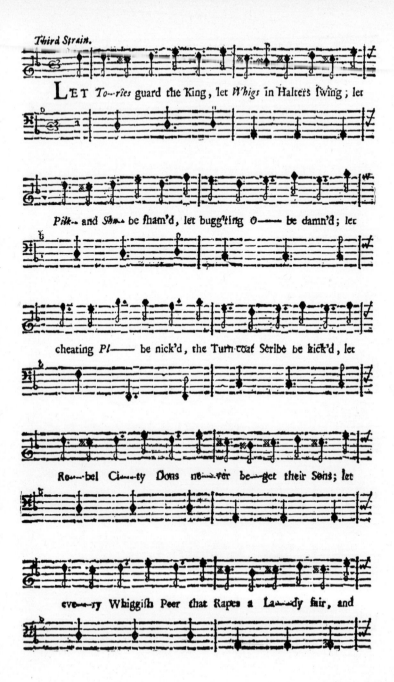

L ET *To---ries* guard the King, let *Whigs* in Halters fwing; let

Pik-- and *Shm--* be fham'd, let bugg'ring *O----* be damn'd; let

cheating *Pl----* be nick'd, the Turn-coat Scribe be kick'd, let

Re---bel Ci---ty Dons ne----ver be---get their Sons; let

eve---ry Whiggifh Peer that Rapes a La---dy fair, and

leaves his on——ly Dear the Sheets to gnaw and tear, be

pu—nifh'd out of hand, and forc'd to pawn his Land, t'at-

tone the grand Af—fair.

Fourth Strain.

GReat *Charles* like *Je—ho—vah* fpares Foes would unking him, and

warms with his Gra—ces the Vi——pers that fting him; 'till

Crown'd with just An——ger tho' Re—bels he fei——zes, this

Hea—ven can Thun——der when e———ver it plea——ses.

THEN to the Duke, fill, fill up the Glaſs, the Son of our

Mar—tyr, be——lov'd of the King; en——vy'd and lov'd, yet

bleſs'd from a-bove, fe-cur'd by an An—gel fafe un-der his Wing.

Song I. [*Several New Songs*, 1684, pp. 13–18]

The Third Strain.

Let *TORIES* Guard the King,
Let *Whigs* in Halters swing;
Let *Pilk* and *Shute* be sham'd,
Let Bugg'ring *Oats* be damn'd: 25
Let Cheating *Player* be Nick'd,
The turn-coat Scribe be Kick'd;
Let Rebel City Dons,
Ne'er beget their Sons:
Let ev'ry *Wiggish* Peer,   30
That Rapes a Lady fair,
And leaves his only Dear,
The Sheets to gnaw and tear,
Be punish'd out of hand,
And forc'd to pawn his Land   35
T'attone the grand Affair.

The Fourth Strain.

Great *CHARLES*, like *Jehovah*,
  Spares those would Un-King Him;
And warms with his Graces,
  The Vipers that sting Him: 40
Till Crown'd with just Anger,
  The Rebel he Seizes;
  Thus Heaven can Thunder,
  When ever it pleases.

Jigg.

Then to the *Duke* fill, fill up the Glass,   45
The Son of our *Martyr*, belov'd of the King;
    Envy'd and Lov'd,
    Yet blest from above,
Secur'd by an Angel safe under his Wing.

The Sixth Strain.

    Faction and Folly,   50
    And State Melancholy,
With *Tony* in *Whigland* for ever shall dwell;
    Let Wit, Wine, and Beauty,
    Then teach us our Duty,
For none e'er can Love, or be Wise and Rebel.   55

II

OLD Tony,

A SONG.   The Tune, *How happy is*
PHILLIS *in Love.*

Let *Oliver* now be forgotten,
   His Policy's quite out of Doors;
Let *Bradshaw* and *Hewson* lie rotten,
   Like Sons of *Fanatical* Whores:
For *Tony*'s grown a Patrician,   5

By Voting Damn'd Sedition,
  For many Years
  Fam'd Politician,
The Mouth of all *Presbyter*-Peers.

Old *Tony* a Turn-coat at *Worc'ster*,   10
  Yet swore he'd maintain the King's Right;
But *Tony* did swagger and bluster,
  Yet never drew Sword on his side;
For *Tony*'s like an old Stallion,
He has still the Pox of Rebellion,   15
  And never was found,
  Like the *Camelion*,
Still changing his Shape and his Ground.

Old *Rowley*'s return'd (Heav'ns bless Him)
  From Exile and danger set free: 20
Old *Tony* made haste to address Him;
  And swore none more Loyal than he:
The King who knew him a Traytor,
And saw him Squint like a Satyr;
  Yet, thro' his Grace,   25
  Pardon'd the matter,
And gave him since the *Purse* and the *Mace*.

And now little Chancellor *Tony*
  With Honour had feather'd his Wing,
He carefully pick'd up the Money,   30
  But never a Groat for the King:
But *Tony*'s luck was confounded,
The Duke soon smoak'd him a *Round-head*,
  From Head to Heel
  Tony was sounded,   35
And great *York* put a Spoke in his Weel.

And now little *Tony* in Passion,
   Like Boy that had nettl'd his Breech,
Maliciously took an occasion
   To make a most delicate Speech;   40
He told the King like a Croney,
If e'er he hop'd to have Money,
      He must be rul'd:
      Oh fine *Tony*!
Was ever Potent Monarch so school'd?   45

The King issues out Proclamation
   By Learned and Loyal Advice;
But *Tony* possesses the Nation
   The Councel will never be wise:
For *Tony* is madder and madder,   50
And *Monmouth*'s blown like a Bladder,
     And *L——ce* too,
     Who grows gladder,
That they the great *York* were like to subdue.

But Destiny shortly will cross it,   55
   For *Tony*'s grown Gouty and Sick;
In Spight of his Spiggot and Fawset,
   The States-man must go to old *Nick*:
For *Tony* rails at the *Papist*,
Yet he himself is an *Atheist*,   60
     Tho' so precise,
     Foolish and Apish,
Like holy *Quack*, or *Priest* in disguise.

But now let this Rump of the Law see,
   A Maxim as Learned in part,   65
Whoe'er with his Prince is too sawcy,
   'Tis fear'd he's a Traytor in's Heart:

Then *Tony* cease to be witty
By buzzing Treason i' th' City,
    And love the King;
    So ends my Ditty:
Or else maist thou die, like a Dog in a string.

70

OLD Tony,

A SONG. The Tune, *How happy is* PHILLIS *in Love.*

SONG II. [*Wit and Mirth: Or Pills to Purge Melancholy,* 1719, II, 283]

III

A SONG.

To Horse, brave boys of *Newmarket*, to Horse,
  You'll lose the Match by longer delaying;
The Gelding just now was led over the Course,
  I think the Devil's in you for staying:
Run, and endeavour all to bubble the Sporters,   5
Bets may recover all lost at the Groom-Porters;
Follow, follow, follow, follow, come down to the Ditch,
Take the odds and then you'll be rich.

For I'll have the brown Bay, if the blew bonnet ride,
  And hold a thousand Pounds of his side, Sir;   10
Dragon would scow'r it, but *Dragon* grows old;
He cannot endure it, he cannot, he wonnot now run it,
  As lately he could:
Age, age, does hinder the Speed, Sir.

Now, now, now they come on, and see,   15
  See the Horse lead the way still;
Three lengths before at the turning the Lands,
  Five hundred Pounds upon the brown Bay still:
Pox on the Devil, I fear we have lost,
  For the Dog, the *Blue Bonnet*, has run it,   20
  A Plague light upon it,
The wrong side the Post;
Odszounds, was ever such Fortune.

The HORSE-RACE; *a Song made and sung to the King at* Newmarket: *Set to an excellent* Scotch *Tune, called,* Cock up thy Beaver, *in four Strains.*

T O Horse, brave Boys of New—mar—ket, to Horse, you'l lose the Match by lon—ger de—lay—ing; the Gelding just now was led o—ver the Course, I think the De—vil's in you for stay—ing: Run, and en—dea—vour all to bub—ble the Sporters, Bets may re-co—ver all lost at the Groom-Porters. Fol—low, fol—low, fol—low,

fol-low, come down to the Ditch, take the odds, and then you'l be

rich; for I'le have the brown Bay, if the blew Bonnet ride, and hold a

thousand Pounds of his side Sir: *Dragon* would scow-er it, but *Dragon* grows

old; he can--not en-dure it, he cannot, he wonnot now run it, as

late--ly he could: Age, Age, does hinder the Speed Sir. Now, now, now they come

on, and see, see the Horse lead the way still; three lengths be—fore at the

turning the Lands, five hundred Pounds up—on the brown Bay still: Pox on the

De—vil, I fear we have lost, for the Dog, the *Blue Bonnet*, has

run it, a Plague light up—on it, the wrong side the Post; Odszounds, was

e—ver such Fortune.

SONG III. [*Choice New Songs*, 1684, pp. 3–6]

IV

Brother Solon's *Hunting* Song. *Sung by Mr.*
Dogget.

Tantivee, tivee, tivee, tivee, High and Low,
Hark, hark how the Merry, merry Horn does blow,
As through the Lanes and Meadows we go.
   As Puss has run over the Down;
When Ringwood and Rockwood, and Jowler & Spring,   5
And Thunder and Wonder made all the Woods ring,
And Horsmen and Footmen, hey ding, a ding ding,
   Who envies the Pleasure and State of a Crown.

Then follow, follow, follow, follow Jolly boys,
Keep in with the Beagles now whilst the Scent lies,   10
The fiery Fac'd God is just ready to rise,
   Whose Beams all our Pleasure controuls;
Whilst over the Mountains and Valleys we rowl,
And *Wat*'s fatal Knell in each hollow we toll;
And in the next Cottage tope off a full Bowl,   15
   What Pleasure like Hunting can cherish the Soul.

V

The Fisherman's Song, *In the First Part, of*
Massaniello. *Set by Mr.* Leveridge.

Of all the World's Enjoyments,
   That ever valu'd were;
There's none of our Employments,
   With Fishing can Compare:
     Some Preach, some Write,   5
     Some Swear, some Fight,

All Golden Lucre courting,
  But Fishing still bears off the Bell;
For Profit or for Sporting.
    Then who a Jolly Fisherman, a Fisherman will be?   10
      His Throat must wet,
      Just like his Net,
    To keep out Cold at Sea.

The Country Squire loves Running,
  A Pack of well-mouth'd Hounds;   15
Another fancies Gunning
  For wild Ducks in his Grounds:
  This Hunts, that Fowls,
    This Hawks, *Dick* Bowls,
No greater Pleasure wishing,   20
  But *Tom* that tells what Sport excells,
Gives all the Praise to Fishing,
  Then who, &c.

A good *Westphalia Gammon*,
  Is counted dainty Fare;   25
But what is't to a *Salmon*,
  Just taken from the Ware:
    Wheat Ears and *Quailes*,
    Cocks, *Snipes*, and *Rayles*;
Are priz'd while Season's lasting,   30
  But all must stoop to Crawfish Soop,
Or I've no skill in tasting.
  Then who, &c.

Keen Hunters always take too
  Their prey with too much pains;   35
Nay often break a Neck too,
  A Pennance for no Brains:

They Run, they Leap,
  Now high, now deep,
Whilst he that Fishing chooses;   40
  With ease may do't, nay more to boot,
May entertain the Muses.
  Then who, &c.

And tho' some envious wranglers,
  To jeer us will make bold;   45
And Laugh at Patient Anglers,
  Who stand so long i' th' Cold:
    They wait on Miss,
    We wait on this,
And think it easier Labour;   50
  And if you'd know, Fish profits too,
Consult our *Holland* Neighbour.
  Then who, &c.

Song V. [British Museum: G.151(115)]

VI

The Second Song in Sir Barnaby Whigg, *to
the Tune of the* Delights of the Bottle.

Farewel my lov'd science, my former delight,
Moliere is quite riffled, then how should I write;
My fancy 's grown sleepy, my quibling is done,
And design or Invention alas I have none;
But still let the Town never doubt my Condition,   5
Though I fall a dam'd Poet I 'll mount a Musitian.

I got fame by filching from Poems and Plays,
But my Fidling and drinking has lost me the Bays;
Like a fury I rail'd, like a Satyr I writ,
Thersites my humour, and *Fleckno* my wit;   10
But to make some amends for my snarling and lashing,
I divert all the Town with my Thrumming and Thrashing.

VII

A Song sung in the Fourth Act

I'le sail upon the Dog-Star,
and then persue the Morning;
I'le chase the Moon 'till it be Noon,
but I'le make her leave her Horning.

I'le climb the frosty Mountain,   5
and there I'le coyn the Weather;

A SONG in the 4th. Act of the *Fool's Preferment*.

'Le Sail up--on the Dog-Star, I'le Sail up-on the Dog-Star, and

then pursue the Morning, and then pursue, and then pursue the Morning; I'le

chase the Moon till it be Noon, I'le chase the Moon till it be

Noon, but I'le make, I'le make her leave her Horning. I'le climb the Frosty

Mountain, I'le climb the Frosty Mountain, and there I'le Coyn the Weather; I'le

tea——r the Rain-Bow from the Sky, I'le tea——r the Rain-Bow from the

SONG VII. [*Orpheus Britannicus*, 1698, I, 122–123]

I'le tear the Rain-bow from the Sky,
and tye both ends together.

The Stars pluck from their Orbs too,
and crowd them in my Budget;   10
and whether I'm a roaring Boy,
let all the Nation judge it.

VIII

A DIRGE.

Sung in the First Part of Don Quixote *by a
Shepherd and Shepherdess.   Set by Mr.* Eales.

Sleep, sleep poor Youth, sleep, sleep in Peace,
    Reliev'd from Love, and mortal Care,
Whilst we that pine in Life's Disease,
    Uncertain, blest less happy are.

Couch'd in the dark and silent Grave,   5
    No Ills of Fate thou now canst fear,
In vain would Tyrant Power enslave,
    Or scornful Beauty be severe.

Wars that do fatal Storms disperse,
    Far from thy happy Mansion keep,   10
Earthquakes that shake the Universe,
    Can't rock thee into sounder Sleep.

With all the Charms of Peace possest,
    Secure from Life's Tormentor, Pain,

The Dirge, or 3d. Song in the 2d. Act. Sung by a
Shepherd and Shepherdess. Set by Mr. John Eccles.

p, poor youth,   flee——p, poor youth,

fleep in peace   poor youth,   poor youth,

sleep   in peace, sleep in peace reliev'd from Love   and

mortal care;   whilst we that pine in Life's disease un-

-cer-tain bless'dless happy are,　　while we　that pine in

life's dif-eaſe, un-cer-tain bleſs'dleſs hap—py are.

Cou—ch'd in the dark and ſi—lent Grave,

Cou—ch'd in the dark and ſi—lent Grave, no ills of Fate,

no ills of Fate thou now can'ſt fear, in vain wou'd Tyrant Pow'r en——

——ſlave, or ſcornfull Beauty be ſe-vere, or ſcornfull Beauty

be ſevere, or ſcornfull Beauty be ſe—vere.

She.

Wa————————rs,

E

With all the Charms, the Cha— —rms of

With all the Charms, the Cha— —rms

pea— —ce, pof—feft fe—cure from life's Torment or Pain.

of peace pof—feft fe—cure from life's Tor—ment or Pain.

Sleep and in—dulge thy felf, fleep, fleep and indulge thy felf, fleep,

Sleep and indulge thy felf, fleep, fleep and indulge thy felf,

fleep and in—dulge thy felf with Reft, nor dream thou e're fhal't rife a—

fleep: In—dulge thy felf with reft, nor dream thou e're fhalt rife a—

—gain; Sleep, and indulge thy self, sleep, sleep and indulge thy self

—gain; Sleep and in-dulge thy self, sleep, sleep and in——

sleep, sleep and indulge thy self, sleep, sleep and in—dulge thy

—dulge thy self, sleep, sleep and indulge thy self, sleep and indulge thy

self with rest; nor dream thou e're shal't rise a———gain.

self with rest; nor dream thou e're shal't rise a———gain.

CHORUS.

Past is the fear of fu-ture doubt, of fu——ture

Past is the fear of fu-ture

doubt, the Sun is from the Dy——al gone, the Sands are su————nk, the

doubt, the Sun is from the Dy——al gone; the Sands are su————nk, are sunk

SONG VIII. [*The Songs to the New Play of Don Quixote.
Part the First*, 1694, pp. 9–18]

Sleep and indulge thy self with Rest, 15
 Nor dream thou e'er shalt rise again.

CHORUS

Past is the Fear of future Doubt,
 The Sun is from the Dial gone,
The Sands are sunk, the Glass is out,
 The Folly of the Farce is done, 20
The Folly of, &c.

IX

A SONG.

Boast no more fond Love, thy Power,
Mingling Passions sweet and sower;
Bow to *Cælia*, show thy Duty,
Cælia sways the World of Beauty:
Venus now must kneel before her, 5
And admiring Crowds adore her.

Like the Sun that gilds the Morning,
Cælia shines, but more adorning;
She like Fate, can wound a Lover,
Goddess like too, can recover: 10
She can Kill, or save from dying,
The Transported Soul is flying.

Sweeter than the blooming Rose is,
Whiter than the falling Snow is;

Then such Eyes the Great Creator   15
Chose as Lamps to kindle Nature;
Curst is he that can refuse her,
Ah, hard Fate, that I must loose her.

A SONG.

Song IX. [*Wit and Mirth: Or Pills to Purge Melancholy*,
1719, II, 188]

X

To CYNTHIA.

A SONG.

Born with the Vices of my kind,
   I were Inconstant too;
Dear *Cynthia*, could I rambling find
   More Beauty than in you.

The rowling Surges of my Blood,   5
   By Virtue now ebb'd low;
Should a new Shower encrease the Flood,
   Too soon would overflow.

But Frailty when thy Face I see,
   Does modestly retire;   10
Uncommon must her Graces be,
   Whose look can bound desire.

Not to my Virtue, but thy Power,
   This Constancy is due;
When change it self can give no more,   15
   'Tis easie to be true.

XI

The PERFECTION,

A New Song.   *To the Dutchess of* Grafton.
Set to Musick by Dr. John Blow.

We all to conqu'ring Beauty bow,
   Its pleasing Pow'r admire;

The PERFECTION; *a new Song to the Dutchess*: *Set to Music by Dr.* John Blow.

E all to conqu'ring Beauty bow, its plea—fing Pow'r ad—

mire; but I ne're knew a Face 'till now, that like yours could infpire.

Now I may fay, I met with one a—ma—zes all Mankind; and

like Men ga—zing on the Sun, with too much Light am blind.

SONG XI. [*A Third Collection of New Songs*, 1685, pp. 16–17]

But I ne'er knew a Face 'till now,
   That like yours could inspire.
Now I may say, I met with one,   5
   Amazes all Mankind;
And like Men gazing on the Sun,
   With too much light am blind.

Soft as the tender moving Sighs,
   When longing Lovers meet;   10
Like the divining Prophets wise,
   And like blown Roses sweet:
Modest, yet Gay; Reserv'd, yet Free;
   Each happy Night a Bride;
A Mein like awful Majesty,   15
   And yet no spark of Pride.

The Patriarch, to gain a Wife,
   Chast, Beautiful, and Young:
Serv'd fourteen Years a painful Life,
   And never thought 'em long.   20
Ah! were you to reward such Cares,
   And Life so long couldst stay;
Not fourteen, but four hundred Years,
   Would seem but as one Day.

XII

A Song.

Bright was the Morning, cool was the Air,
   Serene was all the Sky;
When on the Waves I left my dear,
   The Center of my joy:

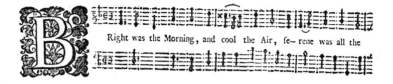

Right was the Morning, and cool the Air, fe--rene was all the

Sky, when on the Waves I left my Fair, the Cen------ter of my Joy; Heaven and Nature

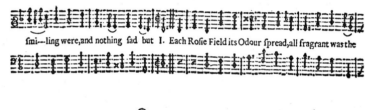

fmi---ling were, and nothing fad but I. Each Rofie Field its Odour fpread, all fragrant was the

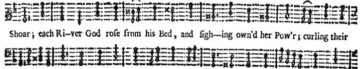

Shoar; each Ri--ver God rofe from his Bed, and figh---ing own'd her Pow'r; curling their

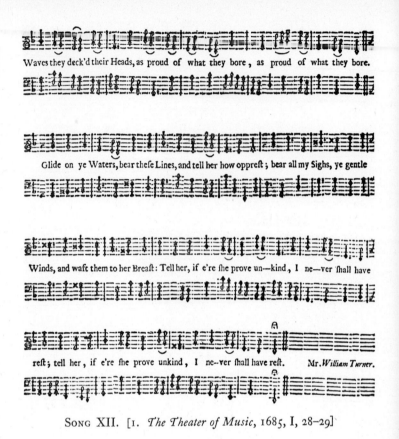

Waves they deck'd their Heads, as proud of what they bore, as proud of what they bore.

Glide on ye Waters, bear these Lines, and tell her how opprest; bear all my Sighs, ye gentle

Winds, and waft them to her Breast: Tell her, if e're she prove un—kind, I ne—ver shall have

rest; tell her, if e're she prove unkind, I ne--ver shall have rest.   Mr. *William Turner.*

Song XII. [1. *The Theater of Music,* 1685, I, 28–29]

Heaven and Nature smiling were,   5
   And nothing sad but I.

Each Rosie Field did Odours spread,
   All Fragrant was the shore;
Each River God rose from his Bed,
   And sigh'd and own'd her power: 10
Curling their Waves they deck'd their heads,
   As proud of what they bore.

So when the fair *Egyptian* Queen,
   Her Heroe went to see;
Cidnus swell'd o'er his Banks in pride,   15
   As much in Love as he:
Cidnus swell'd, *&c.*

Glide on ye waters, bear these lines,
   And tell her how distress'd;
Bear all my sighs ye gentle winds,   20
   And waft 'em to her Breast:
Tell her if e'er she prove unkind,
   I never shall have rest.

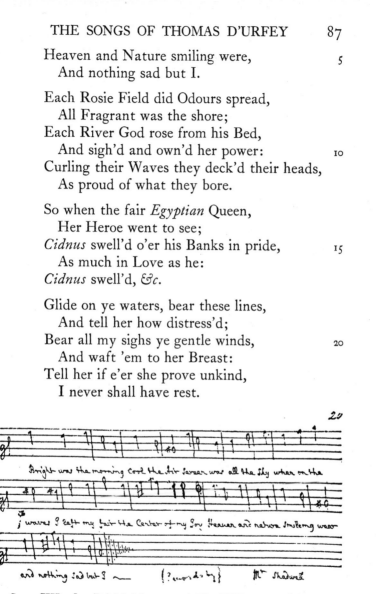

Song XII. [2. British Museum: Addit. MSS. 19759, fol. 20]

XIII

The Mistress: A New Song.

Chloe's a Nymph in flowry Groves,
　A *Nereid* in the Streams;
Saint-like she in the Temple moves,
　A Woman in my Dreams.

Love steals Artillery from her Eyes,　　　　5
　The *Graces* point her Charms;
Orpheus is Rivall'd in her Voice,
　And *Venus* in her Arms.

Never so happily in one,
　Did Heaven and Earth combine;　　　　10
And yet 'tis Flesh and Blood alone,
　That makes her so Divine.

She looks indeed like other Dames,
　With *Atlas* cover'd o'er;
But when undress'd she meets my Flames,　　15
　A Mortal she's no more.

XIV

The Saint at St. James's *Chappel.*

A New Song.

One Sunday at St. *James*'s Prayers,
　The *Prince* and *Princess* by,
I dress'd with all my Whalebone Airs,
　Sate in the Closet nigh.

A new SONG *Compos'd by a Gentleman of* OXON.

Cloes a Goddess in the Groves, a Nai — — — ad

near the streams, an Angel in the Church she moves, a

Wo — man in my Dreams.

SONG XIII. [*The Monthly Mask of Vocal Music*, September, 1709]

I bent my Knees, I held my Book,   5
    I read the Answers o'er,
But was perverted by a Look,
    That pierc'd me from the Door.

High thoughts of Heaven I came to use,
    And blest Devotion there,   10
Which gay young *Strephon* made me loose,
    And other Raptures share.
He watch'd to lead me to my Chair,
    And bow'd with courtly grace,
But whisper'd Love into my Ear,   15
    Too warm for that grave place.

Love, Love, cry'd he, by all Ador'd,
    My fervent Heart has won;
But I grown peevish at that Word,
    Desir'd he would be gone: 20
He went, whilst I, that lookt his way,
    A kinder Answer meant,
And did for all my Sins that day,
    Not half so much repent.

XV

The SERENADE,

A Song *in the Injur'd Princess or a Fatal
Wager, Set by* Colonel Pack.

The Larks awake the drowzy morn,
    My dearest lovely *Chloe* rise,
And with thy dazling Rays adorn,
    The ample World and Azure Skies:

(The Lady Devoted) A New SONG the Words by Mr Durfey

ONE Sunday at St James's Prayers, the Prince and Princess

by, I dress'd with all my Whale-bone airs, sate in the Closset nigh.

I bent my Knees, I held my Book, I read the answers o'er but

was Perverted by a Look, that pierc'd me from the door.

SONG XIV. [British Museum: G. 310 (183)]

Each Eye of thine out-shines the Sun,   5
 Tho' deck'd in all his Light;
As much as he excells the Moon,
Or each small twinkling Star at Noon,
 Or Meteor of the Night.

Look down and see your Beauty's power,   10
 See, see the Heart in which you reign;
No Conquer'd Slave in Triumph bore,
 Did ever wear so strong a Chain:
Feed me with Smiles that I may Live,
 I'll ne'er wish to be free;   15
Nor ever hope for kind Reprieve,
Or Loves grateful bondage leave,
 For Immortality.

XVI

A SONG. *On Young* Olinda.

When Innocence, and Beauty meet,
 To add to Lovely Female Grace,
Ah, how beyond Expression sweet
 Is every Feature of the Face:

By Vertue, ripened from the Bud,   5
 The flower Angelick Odours breeds,
The fragrant Charms of being good,
 Makes gawdy Vice to smell like Weeds.

Oh sacred Vertue, tune my Voice,
 With thy inspiring Harmony;   10
Then I shall sing of rapting Joys,
 Will fill my Soul with Love of thee.

The SERENADE,

A SONG *in the Injur'd Princess or a Fatal Wager*, *Set by* Colonel Pack.

SONG XV. [*Wit and Mirth: Or Pills to Purge Melancholy,* 1719, II, 196–197]

To lasting Brightness be refin'd,
   When this vain Shadow flyes away,
Th' eternal Beauties of the Mind   15
   Will last, when all Things else decay.

XVII

A New Song.   *Translated from the* Italian.

In English.

Ye Beaus of Pleasure,
Whose Wit at Leasure,
Can count Loves Treasure,
   It's Joy and Smart;
At my desire,   5
With me retire,
To know what fire,
   Consumes my Heart:
At my desire,
With me retire,   10
To know what fire,
   Consumes my Heart.

Three Moons that hasted,
Are hardly wasted,
Since I was blasted,   15
   With Beauty's Ray:
Aurora shews ye,
No Face so Rosie,
No *July*'s Posie,
   So fresh and gay.   20
Aurora, &c.

A Song. *On Young* Olinda.

Song XVI. [*Wit and Mirth: Or Pills to Purge Melancholy,*
1719, I, 134–135]

Her Skin by Nature,
No *Ermin* better,
Tho' that fine Creature,
  Is white as Snow;   25
With blooming Graces,
Adorn'd her Face is,
Her flowing Tresses,
  As black as Sloe.
With, &c.   30

She's Tall and Slender,
She's Soft and Tender,
Some God commend her,
  My Wit's too low:
'Twere Joyful plunder,   35
To bring her under,
She's all a wonder,
  From Top to Toe.
'Twere joyful, &c.

Then cease ye Sages,   40
To quote dull Pages,
That in all Ages,
  Our Minds are free:
Tho' great your Skill is,
So strong the Will is,   45
My Love for *Phillis*,
  Must ever be.
Tho' great, &c.

A New SONG sung by Mr. Bartholomew Platt at Sadlers Wells

Ye Beaus of pleasure whose wit at leasure, can count Loves Treasure, it's

Joy and Smart, at my desire, with me retire, to know what fire, consumes my

Heart, at my desire, with me retire, to know what fire, consumes my Heart.

Another Time to the same words

SONG XVII. [British Museum: H.1601(541)]

XVIII

A SONG.

How vile are the Sordid Intrigues of the Town,
   Cheating and Lying continually sway;
From Bully and Punk, to the Politick Gown,
   In Plotting and Sotting, they waste the Day:
All their Discourse is of Foreign Affairs,   5
The *French* and the Wars is always the cry;
   Marriage alas is declining,
     Nay, tho' a poor Virgin lies pining,
Ah Curse of this Jarring, what luck have I.

I hop'd a rich Trader by Ogling Charms,   10
   Into my Conjugal Fetters to bring;
I planted my snare too, for one lov'd Arms,
   But found his design was another thing:
From the Court Province, down to the dull Citts,
Both Cully and Wits of Marriage are shy;   15
   Marriage alas is declining,
     Nay, tho a poor Virgin lies pining,
Ah pox of the *Mounsieur*, what luck have I.

XIX

A SONG.

The Night her blackest Sables wore,
   And gloomy were the Skies;
And glitt'ring Stars there were no more,
   Than those in *Stella*'s Eyes:

A Song in the Marriage-hater match'd.

How Vile are the Sor-did Intregues of the Town, Cheating and Lying con—

—ti—nually fway; From Bully and Punck to the Politick Gown, In Plotting and

Sotting they wafte the day: All their Difcourfe is of Forreign Affairs, The

French and the Warrs is always the cry, Marriage a—lafs is de—cli—ning,

Nay tho' a poor Virgin lyes pining, Ah curfe of this jarring what luck have I.

SONG XVIII. [*Comes Amoris*, 1693, IV, 8]

When at her Father's Gate I knock'd,   5
   Where I had often been,
And Shrowded only with her Smock,
   The fair one let me in.

Fast lock'd within my close Embrace,
   She trembling lay asham'd;   10
Her swelling Breast, and glowing Face,
   And every touch inflam'd:
My eager Passion I obey'd,
   Resolv'd the Fort to win;
And her fond Heart was soon betray'd,   15
   To yield and let me in.

Then! then! beyond expressing,
   Immortal was the Joy;
I knew no greater blessing,
   So great a God was I: 20
And she transported with delight,
   Oft pray'd me come again;
And kindly vow'd that every Night,
   She 'd rise and let me in.

But, oh! at last she prov'd with Bern,   25
   And sighing sat and dull;
And I that was as much concern'd,
   Look'd then just like a Fool:
Her lovely Eyes with tears run o'er,
   Repenting her rash Sin;   30
She sigh'd and curs'd the fatal hour,
   That e'er She let me in.

But who could cruelly deceive,
   Or from such Beauty part;

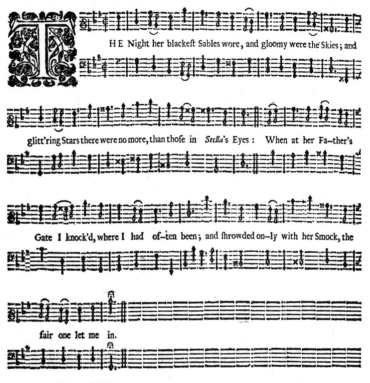

HE Night her blackeſt Sables wore, and gloomy were the Skies; and glitt'ring Stars there were no more, than thoſe in *Stella*'s Eyes: When at her Fa—ther's Gate I knock'd, where I had of—ten been; and ſhrowded on—ly with her Smock, the fair one let me in.

Song XIX. [*Choice Ayres and Songs*, 1683, IV, 8]

I lov'd her so, I could not leave   35
   The Charmer of my Heart:
But Wedded and conceal'd the Crime,
   Thus all was well again;
And now she thanks the blessed Time,
   That e'er she let me in.   40

XX

A SONG.

Sawney was tall and of Noble Race,
   And lov'd me better than any eane;
But now he ligs by another Lass,
   And *Sawney* will ne'er be my love agen:
I gave him fine *Scotch* Sarke and Band,   5
I put 'em on with mine own hand;
I gave him House, and I gave him Land,
   Yet *Sawney* will ne'er be my Love agen.

I robb'd the Groves of all their store,
   And nosegays made to give *Sawney* one;   10
He kiss'd my Breast and feign would do more,
   Geud feth me thought he was a bonny one:
He squeez'd my fingers, grasp'd my knee,
And carv'd my Name on each green Tree,
And sigh'd and languish'd to lig by me,   15
   Yet now he wo'not be my Love agen.

My Bongrace and my Sun-burnt-face,
   He prais'd, and also my Russet Gown;

A NORTHERN SONG.

Saw—ney was tall, and of no---ble Race, and lov'd me bet--ter than a---ny yen; but now he ligs by a---no--ther Lass, and Saw--ney, ne're be my Love a---gen.

I gave him a fine *Scotch* Sark and Band, I put them on with mine own hand; I gave him a House, I gave him Land, yet *Saw—ney* will ne're be my Love a--gen.

SONG XX. [*Choice Ayres and Songs*, 1681, III, 9]

But now he doats on the Copper Lace,
   Of some leud Quean of *London* Town: 20
He gangs and gives her Curds and Cream,
Whilst I poor Soul sit sighing at heam,
And near joy *Sawney* unless in a Dream,
   For now he ne'er will be my Love again.

XXI

The Farmer's Daughter: A SONG.

Cold and Raw the North did blow,
   Bleak in the Morning early;
All the Trees were hid in Snow,
   Dagl'd by Winter yearly:
When come Riding over the Knough,   5
   I met with a Farmer's Daughter;
Rosie Cheeks and bonny Brow,
   Good faith made my Mouth to water.

Down I vail'd my Bonnet low,
   Meaning to shew my breeding;   10
She return'd a graceful bow,
   A Village far exceeding:
I ask'd her where she went so soon,
   And long'd to begin a Parly;
She told me unto the next Market Town,   15
   A purpose to sell her Barly.

In this purse, sweet Soul, said I,
   Twenty pounds lie fairly;
Seek no farther one to buy,
   For I'se take all thy Barly: 20

The last New Scotch Song.

Quld and Raw the North did blow, Bleak in the Morning Early,

all the Trees were hid with Snow dagled in Winters yearly. As I come riding

on the Slow I met with a Farmers Daughter, with Rosie Cheeks and a

bonny Brow, good Faith made me Mouth to water.

SONG XXI. [*Comes Amoris*, 1688, II, 16]

Twenty more shall buy Delight,
  Thy Person I Love so dearly;
If thou wouldst stay with me all Night,
  And go home in the Morning early.

If Twenty pound could buy the Globe,   25
  Quoth she, this I'd not do, Sir;
Or were my Kin as poor as *Job*,
  I wo'd not raise 'em so, Sir:
For should I be to Night your friend,
  We'st get a young Kid together;   30
And you'd be gone ere the nine Months end,
  And where should I find a Father?

I told her I had Wedded been,
  Fourteen years and longer;
Or else I choose her for my Queen,   35
  And tie the Knot much stronger:
She bid me then no farther rome,
  But manage my Wedlock fairly;
And keep Purse for poor Spouse at home,
  For some other shall have her Barly.   40

XXII

Salley's *Answer to* Sawney: *A New* Song.

As I gang'd o'er the Links of *Leith*
  One Morn, was fresh and rosie;
The Birds did sing, the Flowers did breath
  So sweet, I sought a Poesie:

I thought I heard one Sing my praise,   5
    And found 'twas sweet and bonny;
And sounded *Sally* with such grace,
    It must be Charming *Sawney*.

His Daddy, was a Farmer grey,
    That lov'd the Barn and Mow, Sir;   10
Brisk *Sawney* train'd another way,
    Can Pipe, as well as Plough, Sir:
He 'd touch a Flute, and play a Tune
    So soft, so sweet and bonny;
Each *Philomel* that heard fell down,   15
    And died to Eccho *Sawney*.

I often went to Milk our Kine,
    Inspir'd with Love and Folly:
And there he'd Chant a song Divine,
    And close with Lovely *Sally:*   20
The Teats I stroak'd, whence Milk did flow,
    His words too drop'd down Honey;
And ev'ry Note did charm me so,
    I ran half Mad for *Sawney*.

He press'd my Hand and hugg'd my Wast,   25
    A Kiss did then avail too;
And often he my Labour eas'd,
    With carrying home my Pail too:
He ask'd my Dad, for me to Wife,
    Who said, to have more Money;   30
A Neighboring Loon should ease that strife,
    But I resolv'd for *Sawney*.

Then soon my Mother took my part,
    This Girl we must not baulk so;

There's something sad, grows near her Heart,   35
　　Her Face is Pale as Chalk too:
And now 'tis done, the Steeple rings,
　　We each call Joy and Honey;
Whilst I despise the Crowns of Kings,
　　I'm pleas'd so well with *Sawney*.   40

XXIII

A Scotch SONG.

'Twas within a Furlong of *Edinborough* Town,
In the Rosie time of year when the Grass was down;
　　Bonny *Jockey* Blith and Gay,
　　Said to *Jenny* making Hay,
Let's sit a little (Dear) and prattle,   5
　　'Tis a sultry Day:
He long had Courted the Black-Brow'd Maid,
But *Jockey* was a Wag and would ne'er consent to Wed;
Which made her pish and phoo, and cry out it will not do,
I cannot, cannot, cannot, wonnot, monnot Buckle too.   10

He told her Marriage was grown a meer Joke,
And that no one Wedded now, but the Scoundrel Folk;
　　Yet my dear, thou shouldest prevail,
　　But I know not what I ail,
I shall dream of Clogs, and silly Dogs,   15
　　With Bottles at their Tail;
But I'll give thee Gloves, and a Bongrace to wear,
And a pretty Filly-Foal, to ride out and take the Air;
If thou ne'er will pish nor phoo, and cry it ne'er shall do,
I cannot, cannot, &c.   20

'Twas with-in a furlong of *Edenborough* Town, in the Rosie time of year when the

Grass was down; bonny *Jocky* Blith and Gay, said to *Jenny* making Hay, let's

sit a little (Dear) and prattle, 'tis a soultry Day: He long had Courted the

Black-browd Maid, but *Jocky* was a Wagg and wou'd ne'er consent to Wedd, which

made her Pish and Phoo, and cry out it will not do, I cannot, cannot, cannot,

wonnot, wonnot buckle too.

SONG XXIII. [*Deliciae Musicae*, 1696, III, 2]

That you'll give me Trinkets, cry'd she, I believe,
But ah! what in return must your poor *Jenny* give;
 When my Maiden Treasure's gone,
 I must gang to *London* Town,
And Roar, and Rant, and Patch and Paint,   25
 And Kiss for half a Crown:
Each Drunken Bully oblige for Pay,
And earn an hated Living in an odious Fulsom way;
No, no, it ne'er shall do, for a Wife I'll be to you,
Or I cannot, cannot, *&c.*   30

XXIV

A Song

Of noble Race was *Shinking*,
 The Line of *Owen Tudor*,
Thum, thum, thum, thum,
But her Renown is fled and gone,
 Since cruel Love pursu'd her.   5

Fair *Winnies* Eyes bright shining,
 And Lilly Breasts alluring;
Poor *Jenkins* Heart with fatal Dart,
 Have wounded past all curing.

Her was the prettiest fellow,   10
 At Foot-ball or at Cricket;
At Hunting Chace, or nimble Race,
 Cots-plut how her cou'd prick it.

But now all Joys are flying,
   All Pale and wan her Cheeks too,   15
Her Heart so akes, her quite forsakes,
   Her Herrings and her Leeks too.

No more must dear Metheglin,
   Be top'd at good *Montgomery;*
And if Love sore, smart one week more,   20
   Adieu Creem-Cheese and Flomery.

A Song in the *Richmond* Heireſt, or a Woman once in the Right.

SONG XXIV. [*Thesaurus Musicus*, 1693, I, 20]

XXV

The Winchester *Wedding; or* Ralph *of* Redding,
and black Bess *of the* Green.

At *Winchester* was a Wedding,
    The like was never seen,
Twixt lusty *Ralph* of *Redding*,
    And bonny black *Bess* of the *Green*:
The Fidllers were Crouding before,   5
    Each Lass was as fine as a Queen;
There was a Hundred and more,
    For all the Country came in:
Brisk *Robin* led *Rose* so fair,
    She look'd like a Lilly o' th' Vale;   10
And Ruddy Fac'd *Harry* led *Mary*,
    And *Roger* led bouncing *Nell*.

With *Tommy* came smiling *Katy*,
    He help'd her over the Stile;
And swore there was none so pretty,   15
    In forty, and forty long Mile:
Kit gave a Green-Gown to *Betty*,
    And lent her his Hand to rise;
But *Jenny* was jeer'd by *Watty*,
    For looking blue under the Eyes: 20
Thus merrily Chattıng all,
    They pass'd to the *Bride-house* along;
With *Johnny* and pretty fac'd *Nanny*,
    The fairest of all the throng.

The WINCHESTER WEDDING,
Set to the King's Jigg; a Country Dance.

AT Win—che—ster was a Wedding, the like was ne—ver

seen, 'twixt lu——sty Ralph of Rea—ding, and bon——ny black

Bess of the Green: The Fiddles went crowding before, each

Lass was as fine as a Queen; there was a hundred or

more, for all the Country came in. Brisk Ro—bin led Rose so

fair, she look'd like a Lil——ly o'th' Vale; and Ruddy-fac'd

Har—ry led Ma——ry, and Ro—ger led bouncing Nell.

SONG XXV. [*Several New Songs*, 1684, pp. 2–3]

The Bride came out to meet 'em,   25
   Afraid the Dinner was spoil'd;
And usher'd 'em in to treat 'em,
   With *Bak'd*, and *Roasted*, and *Boil'd*:
The Lads were so frolick and jolly,
   For each had his Love by his side;   30
But *Willy* was Melancholy,
   For he had a Mind to the Bride:
Then *Philip* begins her Health,
   And turns a Beer Glass on his Thumb;
But *Jenkin* was reckon'd for Drinking,   35
   The best in *Christendom*.

And now they had Din'd, advancing
   Into the midst of the *Hall;*
The Fidlers struck up for Dancing,
   And *Jeremy* led up the *Brawl:*   40
But *Margery* kept a quarter,
   A Lass that was proud of her Pelf,
Cause *Arthur* had stolen her Garter,
   And swore he would tie it himself:
She struggl'd, and blush'd, and frown'd,   45
   And ready with Anger to cry;
'Cause *Arthur* with tying her Garter,
   Had slip'd his Hand too high.

And now for throwing the Stocking,
   The Bride away was led;   50
The Bridegroom got Drunk and was knocking,
   For Candles to light 'em to Bed:
But *Robin* that found him Silly,
   Most friendly took him aside;

The while that his *Wife* with *Willy*,   55
　　Was playing at *Hoopers-hide*:
And now the warm *Game* begins,
　　The *Critical Minute* was come;
And chatting, and Billing, and Kissing,
　　Went merrily round the Room.   60

Pert *Stephen* was kind to *Betty*,
　　And blith as a Bird in the Spring;
And *Tommy* was so to *Katy*,
　　And Wedded her with a *Rush Ring*:
Sukey that Danc'd with the *Cushion*,   65
　　An Hour from the Room had been gone;
And *Barnaby* knew by her Blushing,
　　That some other Dance had been done:
And thus of Fifty fair Maids,
　　That came to the Wedding with Men;   70
Scarce Five of the Fifty was left ye,
　　That so did return again.

XXVI

Enter a Milk-maid

SINGS.

Chorus.　'Twas in the flow'ry Spring,
　　The Linnet, Nightingale and Thrush,
　　Sate on the fresh green Hauthorn Bush;
And jug, jug, jug, and twee, twee, twee,
　　Most sweetly they did sing.   5

All you that either hear or read,
　　This Ditty is for your Delight;
'Tis of a pretty Country Maid,
　　And how she serv'd a Courtly Knight.
Chorus.　'Twas in the flow'ry Spring, *&c.*　　　　10

This Courtly Knight, when Fields were green,
　　And *Sol* did genial Warmth inspire;
A Farmer's Daughter late had seen,
　　Whose Face had set his Heart on Fire.
Chorus.　'Twas in the flow'ry Spring, *&c.*　　　　15

Oft to her Father's House he came,
　　And kindly was receiv'd there still;
The more be added to his Shame,
　　Since only 'twas to gain his Will.
Chorus.　'Twas in the flow'ry Spring, *&c.*　　　　20

One Evening then, amongst the rest,
　　He came to visit this good Man;
But needs must know where *Clara* was,
　　And heard she was a Milking gone.
Chorus.　'Twas in the flow'ry Spring, *&c.*　　　　25

Then call'd he for his pamper'd Steed,
　　With Pistols at his Saddle Bow;
And to the Meadow rode with Speed,
　　Where she was milking of her Cow.
Chorus.　'Twas in the flow'ry Spring, *&c.*　　　　30

Then down he lights, and ties his Horse,
　　And swore she must his Pain remove;
If not by fair Means, yet by Force,
　　Since he was dying for her Love.
Chorus.　'Twas in the flow'ry Spring, *&c.*　　　　35

The Courtier and Country Maid. A Ballad.

[CHORUS first.]

[*Second Movement, like a* Chorus.]

SONG XXVI. [*Wit and Mirth: Or Pills to Purge Melancholy*, 1719, I, 128]

The pearly Tears, now trickling fall,
　　And from her fair bright Eyes do flow;
But that he heeded not at all,
　　But do's her strait the Pistols shew.
Chorus.　'Twas in the flow'ry Spring, &c.　　　　40

But first pull'd out a fine gay Purse,
　　Well lin'd within, as she might see;
And cry'd, before it happens worse,
　　Be wise, and take a golden Fee.
Chorus.　'Twas in the flow'ry Spring, &c.　　　　45

Oh! keep your Purse, reply'd the Maid,
　　I will not take your golden Fee;
For well you hope to be repaid,
　　And greater Treasure take from me.
Chorus.　'Twas in the flow'ry Spring, &c.　　　　50

A thund'ring Oath then out he sent,
　　That she should presently be Dead,
For were his Heart not eas'd, he meant
　　Point blank, to shoot her thro' the Head.
Chorus.　'Twas in the flow'ry Spring, &c.　　　　55

Then making Haste to seize her went,
　　And laid the Fire Arms at her Feet;
Whilst *Clara* seeing his Intent,
　　Has no recourse to Aid but Wit.
Chorus.　'Twas in the flow'ry Spring, &c.　　　　60

She feigns a Smile, and clinging close,
　　Cry'd out, I've now your Courage try'd;
You've met no simple Country Mouse,
　　My Dear, you shall be satisfy'd.
Chorus.　'Twas in the flow'ry Spring. &c.　　　　65

My Father takes me for a Saint,
    Tho' weary of my Maiden Geer;
That I may give you full Content,
    Pray look, Sir Knight, the Coast be clear.
Chorus.   'Twas in the flow'ry Spring, *&c.*   70

Look out and see who comes and goes,
    And you shall quickly have your Will,
For if my Father nothing knows,
    Then I shall be a Maiden still.
Chorus.   'Twas in the, *&c.*   75

The witless Knight peeps o'er the Hedge,
    As one well pleas'd with what he heard,
When she do's both the Pistols snatch,
    And boldly stood upon her Guard.
Chorus.   'Twas in the, *&c.*   80

Keep off, keep off, Sir Fool, she cry'd,
    And from this Spot of Ground retire,
For if one Yard to me you stride;
    By my sav'd Maidenhead I fire.
Chorus.   'Twas in the, *&c.*   85

My Father once a Soldier was,
    And Maids from Ravishers would free;
His Daughter too in such a Case,
    Can shoot a Gun as well as he.
Chorus.   'Twas in the, *&c.*   90

For Sovereign too, when Foe invades,
    Can on occasion bravely kill,
Not shoot like you at harmless Maids;
    That won't obey your savage Will.
Chorus.   'Twas in the, *&c.*   95

Who when the good old Man, whose Cheer,
  Shew'd welcome, tho' of little Cost,
A Rape thought on his Daughter dear,
  Most grateful way to pay your Host.
Chorus.   'Twas in the, *&c.*   100

Go home ye Fop, where Game's not dear,
  And for half Crown a Doxey get,
But seek no more a Partridge here,
  You cou'dn't keep, tho' in your Net.
Chorus.   'Twas in the flowry Spring. *&c.*   105

At this the Knight look'd like a Mome,
  He prays, he sues, yet vain was all;
She soon convey'd the Trophies home,
  And hung up in her Father's Hall.
Chorus.   'Twas in the flowry Spring, *&c.*   110

NOTES

TEXTUAL NOTES

D'Urfey's texts are in a rather unsatisfactory state. Apparently he was very negligent in supervising the publication of his songs, for misprints abound, and variants occur which have no *raison d'être*. Those of his songs that appear in more than one of his collections often show changes which represent the way he was in the habit of singing them, if not the way he first wrote them. Accordingly, the texts in this edition are from the latest collections published by D'Urfey during his lifetime. This means that most of them are from the 1719–1720 edition of *Wit and Mirth: Or Pills to Purge Melancholy*, which D'Urfey edited for Tonson shortly before his death, and in the first two volumes of which he placed his own songs.

The original spelling and punctuation have been retained, but the old-fashioned long "ʃ" and "VV" have been replaced by the modern "s" and "W". Stanzas are uniformly unnumbered. The following misprints have been corrected, the first form in each case being the reading of the text used in this edition, the second form being the corrected reading.

P.	L.		
54,	[1]	*Thrid*]	*Third*
81,	16	his]	as
84,	11	dividing]	divining
	16	Pride,]	Pride.
94,	20	gay]	gay.
	21	&c]	&c.
98,	1	Sable]	Sables
100,	9	her]	my
102,	39	Hour]	Time
	11	mere]	more
	16	agen,]	agen.
104,	12	Visage]	Village
116,	15	Spring.]	Spring, &c.
120,	103	Patridge]	Partridge

The variants recorded in the following list include only those which affect the actual meaning of the text. The first form in each case is that of the text used in the present edition; the other forms are from earlier collections in which the song in question occurs. The variant readings of "We all to conquering beauty bow" (pp. 82–84) refer to the text on pp. 82–85 of *A New Collection of Songs and Poems*, 1687, and not to the text on pp. 113–114 of that collection. Abbreviations are employed as follows:

A   *The Virtuous Wife*, 1680
B   *A New Collection of Songs and Poems*, 1683
C   *Several New Songs*, 1684
D   *A Third Collection of New Songs*, 1684
E   *A New Collection of Songs and Poems*, 1687
F   *New Poems*, 1690
G   *The Marriage-Hater Match'd*, 1692
H   *The Richmond Heiress*, 1693
I   *The Comical History of Don Quixote . . . Part I*, 1694
J   *The Songs to the New Play of Don Quixote. Part the First*, 1694
K   Scott, *The Mock Marriage*, 1696
L   *Wit and Mirth: Or Pills to Purge Melancholy*, 1719
M   *New Operas*, 1721

P. L.
47, 1   Joy] C All joy
     4   high] E such
    12   his] C the] E the
54, 29   Ne'er] C never] E Never
    35   Land] E Lend
    38   those] C Foes] E Foes
    42   Rebel] C Rebels] E Rebels
55, 55   or] E and
     3   rotten] B rotting] E rotting
56, 10   Old *Tony*] B *Tony*] E *Tony*
    13   Yet] B And] E And
    14   *Tony's*] B *Tony*] E *Tony*
    15   He has] B Had] E Had
    17   the] B a] E a
    18   changing his] B changing both his] E changing both his
    19   *Rowley's*] B *Rowley*] E *Rowley*
    19   Heav'ns] B heaven] E Heaven

56, 21 Old] B Sly] E Sly

22 more Loyal than] B so Loyal as] E so Loyal as

23 who] B that] E that

29 had] B has] E has

30 carefully pick'd] B careful scrap't] E carefully scrap'd

36 great *York*] B *Y—k* soon] E *Y—k* soon

57, 37 And now little *Tony* in Passion] B But *Tony* that frets in his Passion] E But *Tony* that frets in his Passion

38 had] B has] E has

39 Maliciously took an Occasion] B Did late in the house take occasion] E Did late in the House take occasion

46 out] B forth] E forth

48 possesses] B declares to] E declares to

50 For *Tony* is] B Yet *Tony's*] E Yet *Tony's*

51 *Monmouth's* blown] B *M—* blows] E *M—* blows

52 *L—ce*] B others] E others

53 grows] B grow] E grow

54 the great *York* was like to subdue] B Great *Y—k* are like to undo] E Great *Y—k* are like to undo

56 *Tony's* grown] B *Tony* grows] E *Tony* grows

60 he himself is] B is himself] E is himself

62 Foolish] B Sneaking] E Sneaking

65 as Learned in part] B and so we will part] E and so we will part

66 too] B so] E so

67 he's] B is] E is

58, 72 die] B swing] E swing

63, 3 Meadows] G *the Meadows*

8 Pleasure] G *Splendor*

15 tope off a full] G *top off a brown*

69, 9 Storms] I *Storm*

14 Tormentor] I *Torment or*] J Torment or

80, 17 *the*] I *thy*

80, 2 Mingling Passion] B Or thy passion] E Or thy passion

5 must] B does] E does

10 Goddess] B Angel] E Angel

12 The Transported] B When the Ravisht] E When the Ravisht

82, 2 Its pleasing Pow'r] B Its Influence I] E Its Influence I

84, 3 I ne'er knew a Face] B never saw a Star] E never saw a Star

4 yours] B you] E you

84, 9   Soft] B Calm] E Calm
19   a] E of
20   And] E Yet
22   couldst] B could] E could
87, 11   heads] B head] E head
98, 1   of the] G *o'th'*
2   continually] G *perpetually*
4   In] G *With*
5   their] G *our*
8   lies] G *lye*
10   hop'd a rich] G *thought a young*
12   one] G *one that*
15   Cully] G *Cullies*
16   Marriage alas is declining] G *Great are the Sins of the Nation*
17   Nay, tho a poor Virgin lies pining] G *Ah shame on the wretched Occasion*
18   pox] G *Curse*
98, 2   And] B all] E All
100, 7   with] B by] E by
8   The fair one] B this Angel] E This Angel
11   Breast] B Breasts] E Breasts
17   Then! then!] B ah! then] E ah! then
19   knew] B know] E know
20   great] B much] E much
25   oh!] B ah!] E ah!
29   run] B ran] E ran
30   rash] B sweet] E sweet
102, 36   of] B for] E for
37   the] B her] E her
102, 5   fine] A *a fine*
6   mine] A *my*
16   Yet] A *But*
104, 15   unto] F to
108, 7   Brow'd] K *brown*
9   out it will not] K *it ne're shall*
10   monnot] K *wonnot*
12   no one] K *none*
16   Tail] K *Tails*
19   nor phoo] K *and phoo*
110, 28   in an odious] K *an odious*

110,	1	*Shinking*] H *Shinken*
	4	is] H was
	11	Foot-ball or at] H Bandy once and
111,	14	are flying] H defying
	18	Metheglin] H Metheglins
	20	Love] H Loves
112,	5	Fidllers were] C Fiddles went] E Fidles went
	7	and] C or] E or
114,	25	Bride] C Bridegroom] E Bridegroom
	29	so frolick] C frolic] E frolick
	35	reckon'd] C rated] E rated
	39	Fidlers] C Fiddles
	40	*Brawl*] C Brawls
	48	slip'd] C slip'd up] E slipt up
	51	and was] C was] E was
	52	Candles] E Candle
118,	46	Purse] L Gold
119,	78	When] L Whilst
120,	104	cou'dn't] L could not
	107	prays, he sues] L sues and vows

GENERAL NOTES

I. *Joy to great Caesar.* (P. 47)

Text from *Wit and Mirth: Or Pills to Purge Melancholy*, 1719, II, 152–156. "The King's Health," one of the earliest as well as one of the most vigorous and popular of D'Urfey's many loyal songs, was written in 1681 after the election of the Whig sheriffs, Thomas Pilkington and Samuel Shute. Macaulay relates that, following the coronation of James II in 1685 and the subsequent success of the Tories at the polls, the newly elected members of Parliament marched with a band of music and a long train of gentlemen to the City Cross, singing "Joy to great Caesar" (*The History of England*, ed. C. H. Firth, 1913, I, 474). Macaulay describes the song as contemptible in itself (surely an unnecessarily severe judgment), but admits that it was almost as popular at that time as "Lilliburlero" became a few years later. Addison remembered the song in 1713, and remarked, half in mockery, that Charles II "was not a little supported by *Joy to great* Caesar, which gave the Whigs such a Blow as they were not able to recover that whole Reign" (*The Guardian*, No. 67, May 28, 1713). Giovanni Farinelli, the composer of the "ground" to which the song was sung, was an Italian Catholic — hence Addison's jest that D'Urfey made use of Italian tunes and sonatas for promoting the Protestant interest, and turned a considerable part of the pope's music against himself. Alexander Pope parodied the opening of the song in *The Dunciad*: "Joy to great Chaos! let Division reign!" (Bk. IV, l. 54).

The words of "The King's Health" are printed with Farinelli's "ground" in D'Urfey's *Several New Songs*, 1684, pp. 13–18; *Wit and Mirth: Or Pills to Purge Melancholy*, 1707, 1709, IV, 318–322, 1719, II, 152–156; and (four stanzas only) in several

collections of single songs in the British Museum (G.309[34],
G.315[36], and others). The music alone is in *Apollo's Banquet*,
1690, No. 46; and it is used in two ballad operas, *The Beggar's
Opera*, 1728, air LXIII, and *The Restauration of King Charles II*,
1732, air XXIII. D'Urfey's song "Mars now is arming" is sung
to the same tune. The words are in D'Urfey's *A New Collection
of Songs and Poems*, 1687, pp. 137–140; *A Choice Collection of
120 Loyal Songs*, 1684, pp. 179–181; *A Choice Collection of 180
Loyal Songs*, 1685, pp. 300–302; *Deliciae Poeticae*, 1706, pp. 60–
61; *A Collection of Bacchanalian Songs*, 1729, pp. 122–124; *The
Vocal Miscellany*, 1734, II, 8–9, 1738, II, 11–12; *A Complete
Collection of Old and New English and Scotch Songs*, 1735, I,
20–22; *A New Academy of Complements*, 1743, pp. 131–133;
The Aviary, ca. 1750, pp. 298–299; and Addit. MS. 27047, fol. 29.

1   "*Cæsar.*" Charles II.

15   "*Tony's.*" Anthony Ashley Cooper, first Earl of Shaftesbury.

18   "*Tap.*" An allusion to a drain which drew off the fluid
from an unhealed injury in Shaftesbury's body.

24   "*Pilk.*" Thomas Pilkington (*d.* 1691), elected sheriff in
1681, and later three times lord mayor of London.

24   "*Shute.*" Samuel Shute (*fl.* 1681–1682), elected sheriff
at the same time as Pilkington.

25   "*Oats.*" The notorious informer, Titus Oates.

26   "*Player.*" Sir Thomas Player (*d.* 1686), satirized by
Dryden as "railing Rabsheka" in the second part of *Absalom
and Achitophel* (l. 298).

27   "The turn-coat Scribe." Sir Robert Clayton (1629–
1707).

30   "*Wiggish* Peer." Perhaps an allusion to an episode in
the early career of Forde Grey, first Earl of Tankerville, whose
elopement with his wife's sister, the Lady Henrietta Berkeley,
resulted in a famous trial.

45   "the *Duke*." James, Duke of York.

II. *Let Oliver now be forgotten.* (P. 55.)

Text from *Wit and Mirth: Or Pills to Purge Melancholy*, 1719, II, 283–285. This outspoken lyrical attack on the Earl of Shaftesbury was composed in 1681. Nathaniel Thompson, a Tory, undertook to publish it, and was indicted late in the year for doing so (see *The Loyal Protestant and True Domestick Intelligence*, No. 90, December 15, 1681). On April 7, 1682, Thompson was committed to Newgate, but was soon released (*ibid.*, No. 139, April 8, 1682). In his preface to *A Choice Collection of 120 Loyal Songs*, 1684, sig. a3, Thompson declares that he has been imprisoned six times for his loyalty (by which he means his libels on eminent Whigs). "*For near five years,*" he adds, "*I was never free from Trouble, having seldom less than 3, or 4 Indictments at a Session against Me; at other times Information upon Information in the* Crown Office, *which villainous contrivance of their Agents, cost Me at least £500 in Money, besides the loss of My Trade and Reputation; The principal crimes they alledged against Me were,* Let *Oliver* now be forgotten, *a Song*; A Hue and Cry *after* T. O. *when turn'd from* White-Hall; *The* Character of an Ignoramus Doctor; A Dialogue between the Devil and the Doctor; *The* Prisoners Lamentation for the loss of Sheriff *Bethel.*" Thompson's troubles are frequently mentioned in Luttrell's diary.

Both "Old Tony" and "The King's Health" were probably among the songs D'Urfey sang at the great feast held by the Artillery Company at Merchant-Taylors Hall on April 20, 1682, in honor of the Duke of York's return from Scotland. Vivid accounts of the processions before this feast, and of the bonfires and disturbances after it, were printed in the news-sheets of the day. *The Impartial Protestant Mercury*, No. 105, April 25, 1682, supplies the interesting information that "Amongst the rest of their Entertainment, One *Durfy* a Poet sang several *Tory-Songs* and was very much Applauded." The Artillery Company held another feast for the duke on November 28 of the same year (see *The London Gazette*, No. 1777), and D'Urfey seems to have been one of the entertainers on this occasion also (see the titles of two songs in *A New Collection of Songs and Poems*, 1683, p. 74, and *Choice New Songs*, 1684, p. 2).

"Old Tony" was sung to the tune of *How happy is Phillis in love*, which is the same as *An old woman clothed in gray*. It is printed with the air in *A Choice Collection of 180 Loyal Songs*, 1685, pp. 1–3, and also in *Wit and Mirth: Or Pills to Purge Melancholy*, 1719, II, 283–285. The words alone are in D'Urfey's *A New Collection of Songs and Poems*, 1683, pp. 52–55, 1687, pp. 49–53; *A Choice Collection of 120 Loyal Songs*, 1684, pp. 1–3; and *The Nightingale*, 1738, pp. 249–251. An imitation beginning "Let Pickering now be forgotten" is in *A Choice Collection of 120 Loyal Songs*, 1684, pp. 101–103; *A Choice Collection of 180 Loyal Songs*, 1685, pp. 3–5; and *The Roxburghe Ballads*, ed. Ebsworth, 1885, V, 310–314. An answer to D'Urfey's lines, entitled "Oliverus Redivivus," is in Harl. MS. 6914, fols. 65ᵛ–66, in the British Museum.

1 "*Oliver.*" Oliver Cromwell.

3 "*Bradshaw* and *Hewson.*" John Bradshaw and John Hewson, regicides.

5 "*Tony's.*" Anthony Ashley Cooper, first Earl of Shaftesbury.

10 "*Worc'ster.*" The battle of Worcester, September 3, 1651.

19 "Old *Rowley's.*" Charles II.

27 "the *Purse* and the *Mace.*" Shaftesbury was successively lord treasurer and lord chancellor.

33 "The Duke." James, Duke of York.

51 "*Monmouth's.*" James Scott, Duke of Monmouth.

52 "*L—ce.*" John, third Lord Lovelace.

57 "Spiggot and Fawset." See note on l. 18, p. 129.

III. *To horse brave boys of Newmarket to horse.* (P. 59.)

Text from *Wit and Mirth: Or Pills to Purge Melancholy*, 1719, I, 332–333. D'Urfey sang "The Horse Race" to Charles II at Newmarket, where the king was accustomed to divert himself every spring and autumn with horse-races, foot-races, cock-fights, and other sports (see *The Loyal Protestant and True Domestick Intelligence*, No. 24, March 4, 1682; *The Domestick Intelligence*, No. 92, April 10, 1682; and *The Currant Intelligence*, No. 45, September 27, 1681). Edward Howard's play, *The Man of Newmarket*, 1678, act I, refers to Charles's fondness for horse-racing. Addison, in an ironical comparison of Pindar and D'Urfey (*The Guardian*, No. 67, May 28, 1713), declares that the "first gained an immortal Reputation by celebrating several Jockeys in the *Olympic* Games, the last has signalized himself on the same Occasion by the Ode that begins with — *To Horse, brave Boys, to* Newmarket, *to Horse.*" Gay also mentions the song in *The Shepherd's Week* (Wednesday Eclogue).

"The Horse Race" was sung to the tune of *Johnny, cock thy beaver*, and, according to Chappell (*The Ballad Literature and Popular Music of the Olden Time*, n. d., II, 490), made that tune popular. The words and music are found in D'Urfey's *Choice New Songs*, 1684, pp. 3–6; *Wit and Mirth: Or Pills to Purge Melancholy*, 1699, 1707, 1714, I, 87–88, 1719, I, 332–333; and in single-sheet editions in the British Museum (G.312[59], G.315[106]). The tune is used in *The Village Opera*, 1729, air XXV; and the words alone are found in *A New Collection of Songs and Poems*, 1687, pp. 87–88; *The Vocal Miscellany*, 1734, 1738, I, 188; *The Nightingale*, 1738, pp. 217–218; *The Aviary*, ca. 1750, p. 529; and *The Bagford Ballads*, ed. Ebsworth, 1878, I, 80–81 (expanded to three times its original length).

IV. *Tantivee tivee tivee tivee high and low.* (P. 63.)

Text from *Wit and Mirth: Or Pills to Purge Melancholy*, 1719, II, 189. Sung by the actor Dogget as Solon in *The Marriage-Hater Match'd*, 1692, act II. It is in the same mood as "The Horse Race" (p. 59), "The Fisherman's Song" (p. 63), and other sporting songs not included in the present edition. The music is now lost, although it seems to have been known as late as 1739, when the first stanza was altered and used as the third air in *The Raree Show*, a ballad opera by Joseph Peterson:

AIR III.

Tantwivee, twivee, twivee,
  High and Low:
Hark! hark, hark, how the merry,
  Merry, merry Horn does blow:
Whilst over the Bogs, we'll follow th' Dogs;
  For Puss *is gone over th' Plain.*
There's Rockwood, *and* Ranter,
  And Jouler, *and* Spring;
Here's Sweet-Lips, *and* Beauty,
  Make all the Woods ring;
Whilst over the Bogs, we'll follow the Dogs;
  For Puss *is gone o'er th' Plain.*

The words of D'Urfey's song are found in *Wit and Mirth: Or Pills to Purge Melancholy*, 1707, 1712, III, 221, 1719, II, 189; *A New Academy of Complements*, 1715, pp. 104–105; *The New Academy of Compliments*, ca. 1750, pp. 111–113; and *A New Academy of Compliments*, 1784, pp. 111–113.

V. *Of all the world's enjoyments.* (P. 63.)

Text from *Wit and Mirth: Or Pills to Purge Melancholy*, 1719, I, 267–269. D'Urfey was celebrated in his day for his skill as an angler. Addison, in *The Guardian*, No. 67, May 28, 1713,

declares that his old friend "angles for a Trout the best of any
Man in England," and Thomas Baker, in *The Female Tatler*,
No. 26, September 5, 1709, refers to his numerous fishing prom-
enades. D'Urfey often reveals his enthusiasm for fishing in his
writings — for instance in *The Old Mode & the New*, act III,
in which the character Hookem remarks with gusto: "I'll
manage my Hook and Line, and Artificial Fly, upon the River,
and make a Trout of a Yard long leap to me as if he had Quick-
silver in his Guts."

"The Fisherman's Song" was sung in *The Famous History
of the Rise and Fall of Massaniello*, 1700, act IV. Richard
Leveridge's air is found in *Wit and Mirth: Or Pills to Purge
Melancholy*, 1700, 1707, 1712, II, 223–225, 1719, I, 267–269;
in several collections of engraved single songs in the British
Museum (G.151[115], G.305[185], G.310[173], H.1601[353],
and others); and in *The Quaker's Opera*, 1728, air XXI, by
Thomas Walker. D'Urfey's song "When Harold was invaded"
was sung to the same tune. The words alone are in *The Hive*,
ca. 1733, III, 115–117; *The Vocal Miscellany*, 1734, II, 218–219,
1738, II, 177–178; *The Choice*, 1737, I, 110–112; *The Nightingale*, 1738, pp. 35–36; *The Aviary*, ca. 1750, pp. 370–371; and *A
New Academy of Compliments*, 1789, pp. 120–122.

In 1724 *Massaniello* was revived at the Theater Royal in
Lincoln's Inn Fields on July 31, August 4, and August 7. Advertisements in *The Daily Courant*, Nos. 7107, 7110, and 7117,
indicate that the play was revised for these performances, but
call particular attention to the fact that "The Original Song in
praise of Fishing" was retained. *The Daily Courant*, No. 7316,
announces another revival for March 29, 1725, and adds that
"the original Ballad in Praise of Fishing" has been "new set,"
and will be sung by Mr. Leveridge. Another performance is
announced for May 21 of the same year in *The Daily Post*,
No. 1764.

VI. *Farewell my loved science my former
      delight.* (P. 66.)

Text from *A New Collection of Songs and Poems*, 1687, p. 15.
Among D'Urfey's numerous attacks on Thomas Shadwell, this
lyrical satire, sung by the actor Powell in the title rôle of D'Urfey's comedy, *Sir Barnaby Whigg*, is not the least effective.
Shadwell had borrowed extensively from Molière in *The Miser*
and other plays, and he prided himself upon his ability to play
the lute. G. Thorn-Drury (*The Review of English Studies*, 1925,
I, 188–189) takes the reference to Flecknoe in the second stanza
to indicate that Dryden's *Macflecknoe* had circulated in manuscript before its publication in October, 1682. The song was
first printed in *Sir Barnaby Whigg*, 1681, act III, and later in
D'Urfey's *A New Collection of Songs and Poems*, 1683, pp. 11–12.

VII. *I'll sail upon the Dog-star.* (P. 66.)

Text from *New Songs Sung in The Fool's Preferment*, 1688,
pp. 10–12. "I'll sail upon the Dog-star" is still occasionally
heard in recitals of Purcell's music. It is a "mad song," a type
of composition which was extraordinarily popular in the seventeenth century, and which offered to singers a unique oppor-
tunity for the display of their mimic and histrionic talents.
Shakespeare, Herrick, Dryden, Carey, and others wrote "mad
songs," — D'Urfey a half dozen or more. Perhaps the most
popular exemplar of the type was "Tom o' Bedlam," the first
line of which was usually written "Forth from the dark and
dreary cell." It appears in *Le Prince d'Amour*, 1660, p. 169, and
in many subsequent drolleries and anthologies.

"I'll sail upon the Dog-star" is a revision by D'Urfey of an
earlier song which was first published when he was sixteen years
old, and which can hardly, therefore, be from his pen. As found

in *The New Academy of Complements*, 1671, 1713, pp. 305–306, the earlier version runs thus:

> I'le bark against the Dog-star,
>   And crow away the morning,
>   I'le chace the Moon,
>   Till it be noon,
>   And I'le make her leave her horning;
> But I will find bonny *Maud*, merry mad *Maud*,
>   And seek what e're betides her,
>   Yet will I love,
>   Beneath or above,
>   That dirty earth that hides her.
>
> I'le crack the Poles asunder,
>   Strange things I will devise on,
> I'le beat my brain against *Charles-wain*,
>   And I'le grasp the round Horizon;
>   *But I'le find*, &c.
>
> I'le search the Caves of slumber,
>   And please her in a Night-dream,
> I'le tumble her into *Lawrences* Fenn
>   And hang myself in a Sun-beam,
>   *But I will*, &c.
>
> I'le sail upon a Mil-stone,
>   And make the Sea-Gods wonder,
> I'le plunge in the deep, till I wake all asleep,
>   And I'le tear the Rocks asunder.
> But I will find bonny *Maud*, merry mad *Maud*,
>   And seek what e're betides her,
>   Yet will I love,
>   Beneath, or above,
>   That dirty Earth that hides her.

The foregoing version is also found in *Wit and Drollery*. *Jovial Poems*, 1682, pp. 184–185. D'Urfey's effective adaptation was sung in the fourth act of *A Fool's Preferment*, 1688, doubtless by Lyonel (acted by William Mountfort, a fine singer as well as a fine actor), who is represented as going mad in the play. It is not printed in the play itself, but, with Purcell's music, in a supplement appended to it. It also appears with the music in *Orpheus Britannicus*, 1698, I, 122–123, 1706, I, 96–97, *ca.* 1745, p. 60; *A Collection of the most Celebrated Songs & Dialogues composed by ye late famous Mr. Henry Purcell*, *ca.* 1705, p. 7; *Mr Henr. Purcell's Favourite Songs*, *ca.* 1725, No. 22; *The Works of Henry Purcell*, ed. Alan Gray, 1916, XX, 17–19; and in several collections of engraved songs in the British Museum (G.305[178], G.309[70]). The words alone are in *The Hive*, *ca.* 1733, III, 51; *The Vocal Miscellany*, 1734, 1738, I, 229–230; *The Choice*, 1737, I, 95; and *The Tea-Table Miscellany*, 13th ed., 1762, III, 296–297.

VIII. *Sleep sleep poor youth sleep sleep in peace.* (P. 69.)

Text from *Wit and Mirth: Or Pills to Purge Melancholy*, 1719, I, 151. Jeremy Collier vehemently attacked the present dirge in *A Short View of the Immorality and Profaneness of the English Stage*, 1698, p. 197. Collier was offended by the pagan viewpoint implicit in the song, and regarded it as little better than a droll on the resurrection. But Charles Lamb praised the passion of its language (*Specimens of English Dramatic Poets*, 1903, II, 336–337), and John Addington Symonds (*Shakspere's Predecessors in the English Drama*, 1884, p. 57) compared it to the melancholy strains of some of the Elizabethan lyrists. The dirge was set to music by John Eccles and sung by a shepherd and a shepherdess in the first part of *The Comical History of Don Quixote*, 1694, act II. Eccles's music is found in *The Songs to the New Play of Don Quixote. Part the First*, 1694, pp. 9–18. A later anonymous setting appears in *An Antidote against Melancholy*, 1749, pp. 174–176. Joseph Ritson printed the song in *A Select Collection of English Songs*, 1783, II, 150.

IX. *Boast no more fond Love thy power.* (P. 80.)

Text from *Wit and Mirth: Or Pills to Purge Melancholy*, 1719, II, 188–189. "Celia's Victory," as the song is called in some texts, is characteristic of D'Urfey's early manner. It was first printed in *A New Collection of Songs and Poems*, 1683, p. 6, 1687, pp. 8–9, where it is said to have been "*made at* Epsom, *and set by Mr.* Farmer." Epsom was a resort which D'Urfey frequently visited, and where he fought a duel with a musician named Bell (see p. 19). Farmer was the composer of other songs for D'Urfey, notably "The night her blackest sables wore." A setting, presumably Farmer's, is printed with the words in *Wit and Mirth: Or Pills to Purge Melancholy*, 1700, 1707, 1712, II, 221–222, 1719, II, 188–189. The words are in *Wit's Cabinet*, 1703, pp. 142–143, 1737, pp. 145–146, and in Addit. MS. 30303, *ca.* 1690, fols. 2ᵛ–3.

X. *Born with the vices of my kind.* (P. 82.)

Text from *Wit and Mirth: Or Pills to Purge Melancholy*, 1719, II, 307. This song was never popular, but it is pleasing and characteristic. It was set by the eminent Dr. John Blow, whose tune is found in *The Banquet of Musick*, 1689, III, 6–7. The words are in D'Urfey's *New Poems*, 1690, pp. 79–80; *The Nightingale*, 1738, pp. 247–248; *The Aviary, ca.* 1750, p. 84; and *The Universal Magazine*, 1761, XXVIII, 206, which includes a tune different from that by Blow.

XI. *We all to conquering beauty bow.* (P. 82.)

Text from *Wit and Mirth: Or Pills to Purge Melancholy*, 1719, II, 36–37. Dr. John Blow's music may be found in that collection, and also in *A Third Collection of New Songs*, 1685, pp. 16–

17, and *The Devil to Pay*, 1731, air XVIII. In *The Charmer*, 1752, pp. 114–115, the tune is said to be *John Anderson, my jo*. The song was written for the Duchess of Grafton, the beautiful wife of Henry Fitzroy, first Duke of Grafton, a son of Charles II by the Duchess of Cleveland. The earliest version (in *A New Collection of Songs and Poems*, 1683, pp. 86–89) has three additional stanzas, of which the first two follow the first stanza, and the third is placed last. They run as follows:

II.

Like the bright Genious of your Race,
    You spread your Influence,
Your one Sex borrows from your Face;
    And ours from your sence:
Pardon me, since my thoughts I raise,
    With this blest Theam delighted,
For since all loudly speak your praise,
    Then when shou'd I not write it.

III

The glittering Temple of our God,
    Is deckt with forms divine,
But amongst all the heavenly Crowd,
    Is ne're a Face like thine;
The strictest zeal Apostate stands,
    When so much Grace they view,
To heaven they trembling lift their hands;
    But Eyes and hearts to you.

VI.

Thus when eternal kindness flow'd,
    E're wretched *Adam* sinn'd,
Heavens bounteous hand on him bestow'd;
    A lovely Female friend.
I know not how he priz'd that life,
    But this I'me sure is true,
If a true blessing be a Wife,
    She then must be like you.

D'Urfey subsequently dropped these stanzas (and very wisely, too); though both the long and the short versions are printed in *A New Collection of Songs and Poems*, 1687, pp. 82–85, 113–114. Texts of the words are found in *The Compleat English Secretary*, 1714, pp. 143–144; *The Hive*, 1732, I, 149; *The Vocal Miscellany*, 1734, 1738, I, 248–249; *The Cupid*, 1736, pp. 37–38, 1739, p. 42; *The Choice*, 1737, I, 253–254; *The Musical Companion*, 1741, pp. 287–288; *The Aviary, ca.* 1750, pp. 549–550; *A New Academy of Compliments*, 1748, p. 120, 1789, p. 101; *The Tea-Table Miscellany*, 13th ed., 1762, III, 314; and Ritson's *A Select Collection of English Songs*, 1783, I, 183. It was also expanded to eight stanzas and printed as a broadside ballad (British Museum, C.39.k.6[2]).

XII. *Bright was the morning cool was the air.* (P. 84.)

Text from *Wit and Mirth: Or Pills to Purge Melancholy*, 1719, I, 260–261. Ebsworth suggested (*The Roxburghe Ballads*, 1885, V, 568) that this song may be upon Catherine Sedley, daughter of Sir Charles Sedley. Thomas Shadwell, with whom D'Urfey later quarreled, composed a musical setting which is preserved in Addit. MS. 19759, fol. 20. This manuscript belonged to Charles Campelman, dates from about 1681, and contains music by Shadwell for another song, "Fools for themselves will treasures buy," fol. 17. Some years ago D. M. Walmsley (*The Review of English Studies*, 1925, I, 35) hazarded the guess that both the words and the music of these songs are by Shadwell, and acting upon the suggestion, Summers printed them in *The Complete Works of Thomas Shadwell*, 1927, V, 383–384. But Walmsley later withdrew his suggestion (*The Review of English Studies*, 1928, IV, 431). Shadwell's setting can also be found in *The Newest Collection of the Choicest Songs*, 1683, pp. 60–61, and *Wit and Mirth: Or Pills to Purge Melancholy*, 1699, 1707,

1714, I, 132–133, 1719, I, 260–261. Another setting, by William Turner, is in *The Theater of Music*, 1685, I, 28–29. The words alone may be found in D'Urfey's *A New Collection of Songs and Poems*, 1683, p. 5, 1687, p. 7; and also in *Wit's Cabinet, ca.* 1699, pp. 161–162, 1703, p. 133, 1737, p. 137; *The Hive*, 1733, II, 257; *A Complete Collection of Old and New English and Scotch Songs*, 1736, III, 94; *The Choice*, 1737, I, 89–90; *The Aviary, ca.* 1750, p. 72; *The Masque, ca.* 1790, pp. 82–83; *The Roxburghe Ballads*, ed. Ebsworth, 1885, V, 568; and Addit. MS. 30303, *ca.* 1690, fol. 5.

XIII. *Chloe's a nymph in flowery groves.* (P. 88.)

Text from *Wit and Mirth: Or Pills to Purge Melancholy*, 1719, II, 270–271. This song has the distinction of being included in *The Oxford Book of English Verse*, in which the last stanza, either by accident or design, is omitted. It was first published anonymously in *The Monthly Mask of Vocal Music*, September, 1709, with music "*Compos'd by a Gentleman* of Oxon." But the text of this version shows several important variations. It is just possible, therefore, that the song in its original form is not by D'Urfey at all, and that he appropriated and revised it without acknowledgment, as he did on a number of other occasions. The version found in *The Monthly Mask of Vocal Music* reads as follows:

> Cloes *a Goddess in the Groves,*
>   *a* Naiad *near the streams,*
> *an* Angel *in the Church she moves,*
>   *a Woman in my Dreams.*
>
> *Love steal* Artill'ry *from her Eyes,*
>   *The graces point her Charms,*
> Orpheus *is rivall'd in her voice,*
>   *And* Venus *in her Arms,*

Never so happily in one,
  Did heav'n and Earth combine,
And yett tis flesh and blood alone,
  Make her this thing Divine,

She looks like other mortal dames,
  Tell I Unlace her boddice,
But when with fire she meets my flames,
  The wench turn's up a Goddess.

The original song is printed in *The Hive*, 1732, IV, 179; D'Urfey's revision is in *The Nightingale*, 1738, p. 352, and *The Aviary, ca.* 1750, p. 102.

XIV. *One Sunday at St. James's prayers.* (P. 88.)

   Text from *Wit and Mirth: Or Pills to Purge Melancholy*, 1719, I, 10–11, which includes an anonymous tune. W. B. Squire, in his *Catalogue of Printed Music Published between 1487 and 1800 now in the British Museum*, 1912, II, 222, asserts that in some editions the tune is ascribed to D'Urfey, but I have been unable to verify the statement, and I believe that Squire for once has erred. The words and music are found in several collections of single songs in the British Museum (G. 310[183], H. 1601[338], and others). The tune is also used in Ebenezer Forrest's *Momus turn'd Fabulist*, 1729, air XXXII. The words are in *A Complete Collection of Old and New English and Scotch Songs*, 1736, III, 16; *The Cupid*, 1736, 1739, pp. 6–7; *The Choice* 1737, I, 172; *The Aviary, ca.* 1750, p. 303; and *The Tea-Table Miscellany*, 13th ed., 1762, III, 241–242.

   1 "*St. James's.*" The chapel in St. James's Palace.

   2 "*Prince* and *Princess.*" Prince George, afterwards George II, and Caroline of Anspach, his wife.

XV. *The larks awake the drowsy morn.* (P. 90.)

Text from *Wit and Mirth: Or Pills to Purge Melancholy*, 1719, II, 196–197. First printed in D'Urfey's *A New Collection of Songs and Poems*, 1683, p. 12, 1687, p. 16, this attractive song is there said to have been sung in *The Injur'd Princess*, D'Urfey's adaptation of *Cymbeline*. It was not printed with the play, but was probably introduced in act II, scene iv. Captain Pack's setting is found in *Wit and Mirth: Or Pills to Purge Melancholy*, 1700, 1707, 1712, II, 302–303, 1719, II, 196–197. The words alone are in *The Theatre of Ingenuity*, 1704, pp. 148–149; *The Nightingale*, 1738, p. 343; and *The Aviary*, ca. 1750, p. 489.

XVI. *When innocence and beauty meet.* (P. 92.)

Text from *Wit and Mirth: Or Pills to Purge Melancholy*, 1719, I, 134–135, which includes an anonymous melody. Hardly typical of D'Urfey's usual point of view, this song in praise of innocence and virtue transcends in poetical feeling many of his better-known pieces. It is included without the music in *A Complete Collection of Old and New English Songs*, 1736, III, 54, and Ritson's *A Select Collection of English Songs*, 1783, I, 208.

XVII. *Ye beaux of pleasure.* (P. 94.)

Text from *Wit and Mirth: Or Pills to Purge Melancholy*, 1719, I, 11–13, where it is said to be a translation of the following Italian song:

Cant. Italian.

GIOVANI *amanti voi chi Sapete,*
L'Arte secreti d'un crudo Amor;
In Cortesia scoltato un puoro,
L'Ardente fuoco chi marde il Cor.

Egia tre mesi ch'una sitella,
Le giadra Bella ch'ogni lo sa;
Quel sua bel chilio cosci Gallante,
Mi feci amanti di sua bella.

The tune also appears in several collections of single songs in the British Museum (G.305[332], H.1601[541], and others), and in the following ballad operas: *The Lover's Opera*, 1729, air XXV; *The Female Parson*, 1730, air V; *The Jovial Crew*, 1731, air XXV; *The Footman*, 1732, air XLVII; *Penelope*, 1728, air II; and *The Disappointed Gallant*, 1738, air XV. A different tune with the same name (*Ye beaux of pleasure*) was used in John Hippisley's *Flora*, 1729, air II, and also for "A New Song by Capt. I: R.," beginning "You girls so pretty, both young and witty" (British Museum: G. 314[4]). D'Urfey's words are in *The Hive*, 1732, IV, 223–224; *The Choice*, 1733, II, 13–14; *The Vocal Miscellany*, 1734, 1738, I, 96–97; *A Complete Collection of Old and New English and Scotch Songs*, 1735, I, 44–45; *The Nightingale*, 1738, pp. 99–100; *The Aviary*, ca. 1750, p. 640; *The New Academy of Compliments*, ca. 1750, pp. 139–140; and *A New Academy of Compliments*, 1784, pp. 139–140.

XVIII. *How vile are the sordid intrigues of the town.*   (P. 98.)

Text from *Wit and Mirth: Or Pills to Purge Melancholy*, 1719, I, 296–297. Although this is not one of D'Urfey's most interesting compositions, I have reprinted it because of the practical certainty that it was set to music by D'Urfey himself. It was sung by Mrs. Lassells, acting the part of Berenice, in *The Marriage-Hater Match'd*, 1692, act II, and in the following year a portion of the first stanza was sung by Mrs. Bracegirdle, acting the part of Fulvia, in *The Richmond Heiress*, act II. It was published with D'Urfey's tune in *Comes Amoris*, 1693, IV, 8. In *Joyful Cuckoldom*, ca. 1695, No. 30, the music is attributed to Henry Purcell, doubtless erroneously (see *The Works of Henry Purcell*, ed. Alan Gray, 1916, XX, xvii). The words and music are also found in *Wit and Mirth: Or Pills to Purge Melancholy*, 1699, 1707, 1714, I, 99–100, 1719, I, 296–297; and the tune is used in *The Jovial Crew*, 1731, air XLI. The words of the song are printed in *The Compleat Academy of Complements*, 1705, p. 143; *The Compleat English Secretary*, 1714, p. 137; *A New Academy of Complements*, 1715, p. 143; *A Complete Collection of Old and New English and Scotch Songs*, 1736, III, 129; and as a broadside ballad six stanzas in length (British Museum C.39.k.6[12]).

XIX. *The night her blackest sables wore.* (P. 98.)

Text from *Wit and Mirth: Or Pills to Purge Melancholy*, 1719, I, 324–325. Perhaps the finest and most moving of D'Urfey's songs — certainly of his Scotch songs. "The Generous Lover" was formerly thought to be by Francis Sempill of Beltrees (see James Paterson, *The Poems of the Sempills of Beltrees*, 1849, pp. 71–72, 112–114). But Chappell, who has much to say of interest in this connection (*The Ballad Literature and Popular Music of the Olden Time*, n. d., II, 509–511), first showed that it is really by English Tom D'Urfey. Thomas Farmer composed the music, and it made him famous. His air is found with the words in D'Urfey's *A New Collection of Songs and Poems*, 1683, pp. 56–59; *Choice Ayres and Songs*, 1683, IV, 8; *The Newest Collection of the Choicest Songs*, 1683, pp. 25–27; and *Wit and Mirth: Or Pills to Purge Melancholy*, 1699, 1707, 1714, I, 201–203, 1719, I, 324–325. Another tune composed in the eighteenth century is found in *The Musical Miscellany*, 1786, pp. 98–100 (four stanzas only); *The Edinburgh Musical Miscellany*, 1792, I, 156–157; and *The Musical Repository*, 1799, pp. 158–160. Addit. MS. 35276, fols. 2ᵛ–3, contains still another eighteenth-century setting, ascribed to the composer Ignaz Pleyel. The words alone are in *A New Collection of Songs and Poems*, 1687, pp. 53–55; *Wit's Cabinet*, 1703, pp. 125–126, 1737, pp. 131–132; *The Vocal Miscellany*, 1734, 1738, I, 287–289; *A Complete Collection of Old and New English and Scotch Songs*, 1735, I, 122–123; *The Nightingale*, 1738, pp. 316–317; *The Aviary*, *ca.* 1750, p. 488; *The Charmer*, 1752, pp. 25–26; *The Muses Delight*, 1754, p. 266; *The Tea-Table Miscellany*, 13th ed., 1762, II, 123–124; and *The Roxburghe Ballads*, ed. Ebsworth, 1889, VI, 195–196.

XX.　*Sawney was tall and of noble race.*　(P. 102.)

Text from *Wit and Mirth: Or Pills to Purge Melancholy*, 1719, I, 316–317. "Scotch Sawney" was sung in *The Virtuous Wife*, 1680, act III, and at once became widely popular. Chappell (*The Ballad Literature and Popular Music of the Olden Time*, n. d., II, 618–620) cites several continuations, answers, and imitations, one of the most interesting being a ballad entitled "The Loyal Feast designed to be kept in Haberdashers' Hall on Friday, 21 April, 1682, by His Majesty's most loyal true blue Protestant subjects, and how it was defeated. To the tune of *Sawney will never be my love again.*" This ballad opens with an allusion to Shaftesbury ("Tony was small but of noble race"), and deals with a feast which the Whigs tried to hold in opposition to a Tory feast at Merchant-Taylors Hall in honor of the Duke of York. For some account of the celebrations on this occasion, see my note on "Let Oliver now be forgotten" (pp. 55–58). Chappell surmises that Thomas Farmer wrote the tune, which appears anonymously with the words in *Wit and Mirth: Or Pills to Purge Melancholy*, 1699, 1707, 1714, I, 133–134, 1719, I, 316–317, and *Choice Ayres and Songs*, 1681, III, 9. The tune was also used in *Polly*, 1729, air XXX; *The Village Opera*, 1729, air V; *The Chamber Maid*, 1730, air I; and *The Devil to Pay*, 1731, air XXXIII; and it is included in *Apollo's Banquet*, 1690, No. 27. After Ramsay wrote "My Patie is a lover gay," the air seems to have been called, from the title of his song, *Corn rigs are bonny* (see Squire, "Purcell's Dramatic Music," *Sämmelbände der Internationalen Musikgesellschaft*, 1904, V, 560, and Chappell).

Texts of the words are found in *A New Collection of Songs and Poems*, 1683, pp. 39–40, 1687, pp. 35–36; *Wit and Drollery. Jovial Poems*, 1682, pp. 321–322; *The Compleat Courtier*, 1683, pp. 132–133; and *A Complete Collection of Old and New English and Scotch Songs*, 1736, III, 161–162. Four lines of the song are introduced in act III of *The London Cuckolds*, 1682, by Ravenscroft.

XXI. *Cold and raw the north did blow.* (P. 104.)

Text from *Wit and Mirth: Or Pills to Purge Melancholy*, 1719, II, 167–168. "Cold and raw" is a "Scotch song" which illustrates D'Urfey's characteristic style at its best. Impeccable neither in diction nor in meter, it has a fine spontaneity that justifies and explains its enormous contemporary fame. It was first published in *Comes Amoris*, 1688, II, 16, to the tune of *Stingo*, also variously called *Cheerily and merrily*, *Sweet day*, and *The country lass*, but thereafter generally known from D'Urfey's words as *Cold and Raw* (see Chappell, *The Ballad Literature and Popular Music of the Olden Time*, n. d., I, 305–309). At least three answers were written to the song (see *The Roxburghe Ballads*, ed. Ebsworth, 1893, VII, 233), but none of them is as good as the original. Sir John Hawkins (*A General History of the Science and Practice of Music*, 1776, IV, 6–7 n.) tells how Queen Mary, in the presence of Henry Purcell, commanded Mrs. Arabella Hunt to sing "Cold and Raw" to her. Purcell was determined that the queen should hear the tune again, and wove it into the base of a birthday ode which he composed in her honor in 1692.

The words appear with the tune in *Comes Amoris* (cited above) and *Wit and Mirth: Or Pills to Purge Melancholy*, 1700, 1707,

1712, II, 163–164, 1719, II, 167–168. The song without the music is in D'Urfey's *New Poems*, 1690, pp. 132–134; *A Collection of Old Ballads*, 1723, I, 211; *The Vocal Miscellany*, 1734, II, 106–109 (expanded to fifteen stanzas), 1738, II, 76–79 (expanded to fifteen stanzas); *A Complete Collection of Old and New English and Scotch Songs*, 1736, IV, 99–103; *The Nightingale*, 1738, pp. 28–31; *The Aviary*, ca. 1750, pp. 113–115; Ritson's *A Select Collection of English Songs*, 1783, II, 286–287; *A New Academy of Compliments*, 1789, pp. 117–120; *The Busy Bee*, ca. 1790, III, 98–102; and with an additional stanza in *The Roxburghe Ballads*, ed. Ebsworth, 1893, VII, 233. The air was employed in the following ballad operas: *The Beggar's Opera*, 1728, air III; *The Footman*, 1732, air LIX; *Don Quixote in England*, 1734, air XI; *The Whim*, 1734, air XI; *The Jew Decoy'd*, 1735, air III; and *Court and Country*, 1743, air XXXV. Among the many songs sung to the tune of *Cold and Raw* may be cited D'Urfey's "A beau dressed fine" (*Wit and Mirth: Or Pills to Purge Melancholy*, 1719, II, 169), which is an adaptation of "A young man late that lacked a mate" (*Merry Drollery*, ca. 1661, pp. 27–29); and "The Wealthy Farmer's Choice," a black-letter ballad in the British Museum (C.39.k.6[57]). It should be added that "A young man late that lacked a mate" is sung to the tune of *Cold and raw* in *Wit and Mirth: Or Pills to Purge Melancholy*, 1712, III, 224–226, but that it is provided with a new air by Turner in *The Monthly Mask of Vocal Music*, July, 1710.

XXII. *As I ganged o'er the links of Leith.*   (P. 106.)

Text from *Wit and Mirth: Or Pills to Purge Melancholy*, 1719, II, 240. This is a characteristic "Scotch song," though never very popular, and excessively irregular in its rhetoric. The original tune has not survived, but Mrs. Franklin is said to have sung it at Vauxhall, with music by James Hook, in 1801 (Addit. MS. 28971, fols. 162–165^{v}).

XXIII. 'Twas within a furlong of Edinburgh town.
(P. 108.)

Text from *Wit and Mirth: Or Pills to Purge Melancholy*, 1719, I, 326–327. An altered version beginning "Within a mile of Edinburgh town" is still familiar in Scotland. Chappell, in his invaluable work *The Ballad Literature and Popular Music of the Olden Time*, n. d., II, 611, cites *A second Tale of a Tub*, which tells how the roaring boys of 1715 "split their throats in hollowing out *Bonny Dundee*, *Valiant Jockey*, *Sawney was a dowdy lad* and *'Twas within a furlong of Edinborough town*." The song was first sung in a play by Thomas Scott (*The Mock Marriage*, 1696, act III). The lively melody has been attributed to Henry Purcell, almost certainly erroneously (see *The Works of Henry Purcell*, ed. Alan Gray, 1916, XX, xx); but in Addit. MS. 22099, fol. 9 (*ca.* 1696), it is attributed to Jeremiah Clarke. The words and music are in *Deliciae Musicae*, 1696, III, 2–3; *Wit and Mirth: Or Pills to Purge Melancholy*, 1699, 1707, 1714, I, 233–234, 1719, I, 326–327; *A Collection of new Songs . . . by Several Masters*, ca. 1710, No. 20; Addit. MS. 25074, fol. 17; Addit. MS. 25075, fol. 29^v; and in several collections of single songs (British Museum G. 312[51], G. 315[83, 164], and others). The tune appears in Addit. MS. 24889, fols. 24^v, 49^v, 69^v, and 92^v (arranged for four voices), and in the following ballad operas: *Polly*, 1729, air V; *The Village Opera*, 1729, air XXVI; *The Lover's Opera*, 1729, air VII; *The Chamber Maid*, 1730, air XV; *The Devil to Pay*, 1731, air XXX; and *The Footman*, 1732, air XXXIII.

An eighteenth-century setting by James Hook was "Sung by Mrs. Wrighten at Vauxhall," according to *The Bull-Finch*, *ca.* 1780, pp. 373–374. Hook's setting also appears in *The Musical Miscellany*, 1786, pp. 272–274; *The Edinburgh Musical Miscellany*, 1793, II, 306–307; and *The Vocal Magazine*, 1798, II, No. 23. The words of the song are in *The Compleat English*

Secretary, 1714, p. 135; *A New Academy of Complements*, 1715, pp. 142–143; *The Hive*, 1733, II, 240–241; *The Vocal Miscellany*, 1734, I, 144–145, II, 190–191, 1738, I, 144–145; *A Complete Collection of Old and New English and Scotch Songs*, 1735, I, 27–28; *The Choice*, 1737, I, 57–58; *A New Academy of Compliments*, 1748, pp. 113–114, 1784, p. 138, 1789, p. 96; *The New Academy of Compliments*, ca. 1750, p. 138; *The Busy Bee*, ca. 1790, III, 182–183; and Addit. MS. 28095, fol. 54. It also was published as a broadside ballad, a copy being in the collection of the Earl of Crawford (*Bibliotheca Lindesiana Catalogue of a Collection of English Ballads*, 1890, No. 1221).

XXIV. *Of noble race was Shinken.* (P. 110.)

Text from *Wit and Mirth: Or Pills to Purge Melancholy*, 1719, II, 172. This should be compared with the numerous "Scotch songs" written by D'Urfey and his contemporaries. It was originally sung to the accompaniment of a harp by Shinken (played by Bowman) in *The Richmond Heiress*, 1693, act IV (printed on sig. A3ᵛ), and the words and music appear in *Thesaurus Musicus*, 1693, I, 20; *Wit and Mirth: Or Pills to Purge Melancholy*, 1699, 1707, 1714, I, 311, 1719, II, 172; and as a single song (British Museum G. 310[188] and H. 1601[330]). The tune is used in several ballad operas: *The Beggar's Opera*, 1728, air XXXI; *The Humours of the Court*, 1732, air XXI; *The Wanton Jesuit*, 1733, air XVII; and *Court and Country*, 1743, air XII. It is also found in the following manuscripts: Addit. MS. 35043, fol. 6ᵛ (1694–1697); Addit. MS. 24889, fols. 21ᵛ, 46ᵛ, 66ᵛ, 89ᵛ; and Addit. MS. 35274, fols. 30ᵛ–31ᵛ. In the last it is described as a Welsh air, and is said to have been harmonized by the German composer, Joseph Haydn.

The words have sometimes been erroneously ascribed to Dryden (see *Notes and Queries*, 3d series, 1867, XI, 316, 348). They are found in *Deliciae Poeticae*, 1706, p. 152 (with a Latin translation); *The Vocal Miscellany*, 1734, II, 210–211, 1738, II, 170; *A Complete Collection of Old and New English and Scotch Songs*, 1736, IV, 61–62; *Bacchus and Venus*, 1737, p. 112; *The Musical Companion*, 1741, pp. 242–243; *The Aviary*, ca. 1750, p. 375; *The Muses Delight*, 1754, p. 271; Addit. MS. 30162, fols. 42ᵛ–43 (with Greek and Latin translations by the Reverend John Davies, chaplain to the Earl of Northumberland); Addit. MS. 15023, fol. 74ᵛ; and Harl. MS. 2127, fol. 40.

XXV. *At Winchester was a wedding.* (P. 112.)

Text from *Wit and Mirth: Or Pills to Purge Melancholy*, 1719, I, 276–278. D'Urfey is doubtless here imitating Suckling's more familiar "Ballad of a Wedding." He himself sang "The Winchester Wedding" before Charles II at Winchester, and later wrote a sequel to it entitled "The Winchester Christening" (*A Third Collection of New Songs*, 1685, pp. 7–9). Addison, in *The Guardian*, No. 67, May 28, 1713, pokes gentle fun at D'Urfey's rustic songs, of which "The Winchester Wedding" is a characteristic specimen, and truthfully observes that the individuals he has sung about — "*Pretty* Peg *of* Windsor, Gillian *of* Croyden, *with* Dolly *and* Molly, *and* Tommy *and* Johnny" — would fill a playhouse and make a good benefit night.

The tune was at first called *The King's jig*, but later, because of the popularity of D'Urfey's words, it became known as *The Winchester Wedding* (see Chappell, *The Ballad Literature and Popular Music of the Olden Time*, n. d., II, 495–496). The words and music are found in D'Urfey's *Several New Songs*, 1684, pp. 2–4; *A Choice Collection of 180 Loyal Songs*, 1685, pp. 131–133; *Wit and Mirth: Or Pills to Purge Melancholy*, 1699, 1707, 1714, I, 22–24, 1719, I, 276–278; and in a collection of single songs in the British Museum (H.1601[19]). The words alone are in D'Urfey's *A New Collection of Songs and Poems*, 1687, pp. 124–127; *A Choice Collection of 120 Loyal Songs*, 1684, pp. 136–139;

The Hive, ca. 1733, III, 180–182; *The Vocal Miscellany,* 1734, 1738, II, 112–114; *A Complete Collection of Old and New English and Scotch Songs,* 1735, I, 37–39; *The Choice,* 1737, I, 121–123; *The Aviary, ca.* 1750, pp. 9–10; *The Masque, ca.* 1790, pp. 254–256; Ritson's *Ancient Songs,* 1790, pp. 295–298; and *The Roxburghe Ballads,* ed. Ebsworth, 1893, VII, 208–209. The air was used in many ballad operas, including *The Quaker's Opera,* 1728, air XXIV; *The Fashionable Lady,* 1730, air XL; *The Jovial Crew,* 1731, air XXI; *The Highland Fair,* 1731, air L; *The Devil of a Duke,* 1732, air X; *The Mock Doctor,* 1732, air II; *The Wanton Jesuit,* 1733, air XII; and *The Lover his own Rival,* 1736, air II.

XXVI. *All you that either hear or read.* (P. 115.)

Text from *The Two Queens of Brentford: Or, Bayes no Poetaster,* 1721, act IV. *The Two Queens of Brentford* is a rather puzzling work which D'Urfey printed in *New Operas,* 1721, his last published volume. In his preface he calls the play a "*Musical Farce, or Comical Opera,*" "*a piece of Humour and Grotesque Wit,*" "*design'd as the second Part of the former Rehearsal, wrote by the late Duke of* Buckingham, *and others; but not design'd so Satyrical upon Poetry as that was against Mr.* Dryden, *but intended rather against the Criticks.*" It was once nearly produced, D'Urfey says, and he adds that the reader should find much diversion in it, "*particularly in the variety of Dialogues and Songs, which I have been told, by good Judges, are not indifferent.*" The songs, indeed, are the most important element in the play, and the truth of the matter is that D'Urfey was here groping for the ballad-opera formula which Gay afterwards hit upon. As Whincop remarks (*A Compleat List of all the English Dramatic Poets,* 1747, p. 225), he lived before his time, "for had he lived till the Ballad-Operas came in Vogue, what a Figure he must have made?"

The present ballad is a burlesque of the street-ballads and broadsides of the seventeenth century, with traces of what we now regard as the genuine folk-ballad — a type of composition handed down by word of mouth from an earlier age, and thoroughly familiar to D'Urfey. It was introduced into the play in order to point a contrast between native English song and Italian opera (of which D'Urfey was a persistent opponent), for when it is finished, the character Bayes remarks that "the Relish and Story in't shall vie with all the Opera Trillo's in *Europe*, egad." It will be remembered that Italian opera was one of the objects of Gay's satire in *The Beggar's Opera* a few years later. The cheerful refrain is a noteworthy feature of D'Urfey's ballad. In the play itself, the ballad is sung by a milkmaid; but in *Wit and Mirth: Or Pills to Purge Melancholy*, 1719, I, 128–131, which includes an anonymous melody, it is arranged as a dialogue between two rustics, Bombuy and Doppa, Bombuy singing the first two lines of each stanza, and Doppa the last two. There is also, in this text, an additional stanza after the fifth stanza, as follows:

> Her pretty Hands that stroak'd the Teats,
> From whence the Milk down streaming came,
> Inform'd his Thoughts of other Sweets,
> That more encreas'd his raging Flame.
> *'Twas in the flowry Spring*, &c.

INDEXES

INDEX OF FIRST LINES

INDEX OF NAMES AND TITLES